WALLY'S WORKSHOP

by Wally Bruner

with Natalie Bruner

SIMON AND SCHUSTER, NEW YORK

SBN 671-21523-X Casebound
SBN 671-21908-1 Paperback
Library of Congress Catalog Card Number: 72-90387
Designed by Jack Jaget
Manufactured in the United States of America

　　2　3　4　5　6　7　8　9　10 Casebound
1　2　3　4　5　6　7　8　9　10 Paperback

To Natalie,
who complains about the messes,
asks all sorts of embarrassing questions,
but still is the best partner and wife
any do-it-yourselfer could desire.
Besides, she is the best stripper in the business.

Contents

PART II: INDOORS—THE FURNISHINGS

PART III: OUTDOORS

INTRODUCTION

Let me say at the outset that there are at least twenty different ways to do every job. On some jobs I will tell you about all twenty, but on most of the tasks I have undertaken I have learned that, for me at least, there is one way better than the rest. What I hope will benefit you is my own personal experience in doing each project. This book describes no task that I have not tried and completed to my own satisfaction.

I might also add that "to my satisfaction" does not necessarily mean to my wife, Natalie's! I only promise you one thing. If you attempt a job as described in this book, you will be able to finish it and I will be happy with what you have done. I can't and won't try to speak for your wife; that's your problem. To the ladies who may want to follow my directions, I can only offer encouragement and gratitude. My wife didn't learn to tie her own shoes until she graduated from college, but today she is the best stripper in the business . . . I refer to stripping paint, of course.

Women do tend to be a bit more particular in performing a task. It usually takes them forever to get it done, but when it is completed, it's a lot closer to perfection than when the average man tackles the same job. So, ladies, don't hesitate to try your wings! You can wallpaper, install ceramic tile and do dozens of other tasks and still keep your femininity intact. Even if you don't wish to do the job yourself, you should still read this book so you can heckle your husband as he works.

Perhaps I should explain how I was trapped into becoming a do-it-yourselfer. I was dragged, kicking and screaming, by my hundred-and-twenty-pound wife into the most dilapidated old mansion you'll ever see! Weeks of wifely pleading and tears resulted in our purchase of this monstrosity, which, by the way, took every available nickel we had just to make the down payment.

I'll never forget the night we moved in! All of the furniture from our one-bedroom apartment was unceremoniously dumped into the large living room of the eighteen-room house. A bare bulb was hanging from the ceiling. There was no water or heat. Mice, squirrels and bats were protesting our presence. Plaster was hanging from the ceiling; windowpanes were missing; the roof leaked and even the outdoor john seemed to be imitating the leaning tower of Pisa. And there was Natalie, saying something like "Isn't this marvelous!" Her attitude changed rapidly the next morning as she walked through three-foot-high weeds to the privy.

But alas, since all of our money was already spent, we had no choice as to who was going to make the place habitable. We had to do it ourselves, and for the next two and one-half years, we did! Morning, noon and night. Every floor, wall and ceiling had to be completely restored. Eight layers of calcimine paint covered the walls. One-hundred-year-old black varnish was on the floors. And the only heat in the house was from six smoking fireplaces, each with its own combination of bats, birds and squirrels. No one had lived in the house for nine years, so we were also well endowed with grime. The beautiful ivy that covered the outside stone walls turned out to be of the poison variety. Who could ask for a better dream house for a couple who had been married less than one month!

After a two-and-one-half-year ordeal, we sold the house 95 percent restored to its original splendor. We made money on the restoration and enjoyed doing most of it. I'm always asked, "Would you do it again?" and the answer is always the same: **"No."**

But what we learned doing it is what this book is all about. Believe me, I've been there, and if you are planning that kind of trip, may I suggest you turn the page—and I wish you Bon Voyage!

Part I

INDOORS
—THE SETTING

1 DRYWALL AND SPACKLE

You don't really need brains for this sort of job. In fact, its probably easier if you don't have them! All you need is a little muscle and an understanding wife who will help you clean up the mess after you've finished. For years I found it difficult to successfully patch a plasterboard or gypsum-board wall. Natalie would pound a nail into the wall to hang a picture, then change her mind about where she wanted it, and I'd end up with an ugly hole to fill. I'd go down and buy a can of ready-mixed patching plaster and apply it to the damaged part of the wall—and in a couple of days the patching material would shrink and the damaged part would stick out like a sore thumb. Maybe that has also happened to you! Such experiences are what kept me from attempting to install new drywall in an addition to our house. I figured that if I didn't have the talent to patch a small hole in a wall, I'd never be able to drywall and spackle and have it look halfway decent.

I was wrong! In desperation, after watching a master drywall man at work, I finally tackled the job. Hear me out before you give up and throw up your hands, because you can do it, and do it well.

Drywall material comes in a variety of thicknesses, but the most common thickness used is ⅜". This type of drywall, or gypsum board, is a plasterlike material compressed between two heavy sheets of paper. It comes in sheets 4' x 8', designed to be installed over two-by-four studding spaced either 24" or 16" on center. It is always nailed to the studding with drywall nails, which are about 1¼" long with a big flat head. The head of the nail should press very tightly into the surface of the drywall. You should not break the paper on the drywall when the nail is driven in, but it should be slightly recessed into the surface. Nail at about 6" intervals into the two-by-four studding, and continue until you have applied all the drywall in the room or partition you are working on.

After the drywall has been nailed in place you will have joints, which are where each sheet of drywall joins another, and these cracks must be filled for a smooth, continuous surface. You must also cover the nails. Although the process is called "spackling," I like to use a product called "drywall compound" instead of the product called "spackle." This compound is premixed and comes in cans up to five gallons in size. Take off the lid and it's ready to use. You will also need drywall tape, which is simply paper tape approximately 2" wide. Don't be surprised when you discover that the tape has no adhesive! The paper tape is designed to strengthen the joints of the drywall and will be pressed into the wet compound that will be applied to the wall. You will also need a wide drywall knife. It's a broader version of a putty knife, usually 4" to 6" in width. Get the more expensive one, because it's made of better steel and the blade has a better flex action, which is needed for a smooth job.

Start your spackling on the nails. Dip the knife into the can of compound and get a glob of it on the knife. Wipe

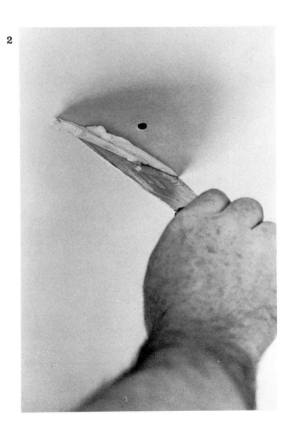

1

2

1 Drywall is first nailed in place with drywall nails. The head of the nail should not break the paper covering on the panel of drywall. However, the head and the area around it should be slightly recessed. This is one time in carpentry when you want a hammer blow to show.

2 You must also coat over every nail that holds the drywall in place. Be skimpy with the compound, because it is doubtful that one coat of material will do the job. Leaving a big glob will result in more sanding than you will like.

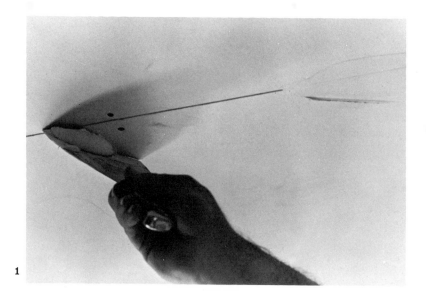

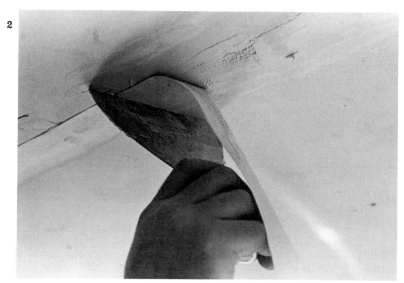

1 On joints between panels, I first fill the cracks with a wide-blade knife, as shown here.

2 Start the tape at one end of the joint and press it into place with a wide-blade knife. Press hard, and the excess compound will be forced out along the edge of the knife. The tape reinforces the joint and is essential for a good job.

the knife over the nailhead with one smooth motion, and presto!—the nail has disappeared. It won't be perfect the first time you do it, but practice a couple of times on this first attempt. Try varying amounts of pressure on the knife as you draw it over the nailhead. Change the angle slightly until the compound flows onto the surface of the drywall without ragged edges. "Wipe" the compound in one direction, then cross-wipe it from another direction. You'll get the knack of it in a few minutes. It is important to achieve a smooth look before the compound dries. Once it is dry, the only way you can correct imperfections is to lightly sand the surface, or go over it with another coat of compound.

Now that you have the hang of it, you're ready to tape a joint. With a liberal amount of compound on your knife, apply the compound down the joint in a layer about ⅛″ thick and 2″–3″ wide. You can even smear it on with a little abandon! Next, tear off a piece of the paper tape that will stretch the entire length of the joint from ceiling to floor. Press the tape into the compound with your fingers so that it will stick to the compound. Don't try to smooth it out; just press it up. Next, take your knife and, starting at the ceiling, run the knife the entire length of the tape. This will press the tape into the compound and give you a smooth joint. The idea of this process is to seal the tape into the compound so that it will not show after the compound has dried. If the edges of the tape show any signs of bulging, give the entire length of the tape another thin coat of compound.

There is one other tool you will need if you have a corner to tape. I am referring to a special corner knife. The paper tape is designed so that it can be folded to fit into a corner. You apply the compound first, giving a liberal coat to both sides of the corner. Next, crease the tape at right angles and press it into the corner. The corner knife is just what the name implies. It has a right-angle blade which fits perfectly into a corner and seals the tape into the compound on both walls simultaneously. This same knife also works very well where the ceiling joins the wall. Let the compound dry overnight. Touch up the rough spots by lightly sanding with fine sandpaper. If you want a smooth wall, it's ready to paint. If you want a textured surface, you have more work ahead of you.

To put a textured surface on drywall is no more difficult than taping joints. In fact, it's easier. You may use the same drywall compound or you can use a sand-mix compound, which will give you a grainier surface. Your paint dealer will be happy to explain what he has available. I use a plasterer's trowel for texturing a wall. This tool is a rectangle about 5″–6″ wide and 10″–12″ long. It has a handle and is made of steel. All you really do is smear on whatever mix you decide to use. You can smear it on in swirls, or whatever. It's messy, but simple. The thickness of the coat is determined by the pattern you're after. When I texture, I use what I call a "skim" coat: just enough to cover the surface and really not much thicker than a coat of paint.

But now, back to the original problem. Patching drywall is no tremendous job anymore! If one of the kids pushes his fist through the wall and you have a big hole to patch, it's simple. Fill the hole with crushed newspapers—not so that the newspapers protrude from the hole, but so that they will act as a "backboard" to hold the drywall compound. Next, put a layer of the compound over the newspaper-stuffed hole. Let it dry. Give it another coat of compound and you've solved your problem. Nail holes can be filled the same way, only you won't need the newspaper. Using your drywall knife, fill the hole with compound. Let it dry. It will shrink some and you'll still see the imperfection in the wall. Then give it another skim coat of compound and it will be repaired.

Plaster cracks and drywall cracks are not that tough either. If a hairline crack is really bugging you, here's what you do. Gouge out the crack in the wall its entire length with something like a beer-can opener. The crack should be at least ⅛″ wide, so that you press the compound into the crack instead of just over the surface. Take a wet sponge, or an old spray-type bottle filled with water, and moisten the crack before you apply the compound. This will prevent the wallboard or plaster from drawing the moisture out of the compound too quickly. When that happens, the compound does not dry slowly enough and will tend to crumble and crack. After the damaged part of the wall has been moistened, spread the compound into the crack with your knife, let it dry, then give it a skim coat of compound and it's repaired. Don't be in too big a hurry to give it the second coat. Let it dry thoroughly and shrink all it's going to shrink before you give the crack its final coat of compound. In some cases you may need yet another skim coat, but you'll learn as you go along— and as I always say, "You can do it, if you try!"

Natalie's Notes

I watched Wally do all the things he wrote about in this chapter and it was positively fascinating. Which should give you some idea of how I regard my role in the entire process.

Actually, I have plugged a few nail holes, but drywalling an entire room I leave to my most capable husband.

I think the thought of putting in new walls is far more fearsome than the actual doing. I know Wally was delighted with and proud of the excellent job he did. Three cheers for Wally!

Maybe if your wall has a crack like this it's time to move? There is an alternative, because even a bad plaster crack like this one can be repaired in as little as twenty minutes.

1

2

3

1 First, remove all the loose plaster from the area you are going to repair.

2 Moisten the edges of the old plaster and lath with water before you apply the compound.

3 I use ready-mixed drywall compound for this sort of work, and as you can see, you just smear it in!

1   2

1 Don't try to get it perfectly smooth . . . yet!
2 This stuff is called paper drywall tape. It's about 2″ wide, and I'm using it to reinforce the badly cracked corner. First, fold and crease the tape.
3 Start at the top of the crack and gently push the tape into the corner over the fresh compound. (Don't give the compound time to dry—do it right away!)
4 After the tape is stuck to the wall, immediately use a corner knife to seal the tape and the compound evenly and also smooth and feather the edges with one quick stroke. Again, don't try to make it perfectly smooth, because when the compound dries it may crack just a bit because of the thickness of the filling.
5 Looks better, doesn't it? If you do a perfect job, you won't even have to sand it. Just in case, fine sandpaper takes all the little bumps out of the plaster after it has dried.

3   4

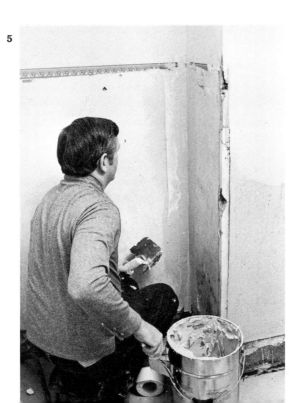

5

25

2 WALLPAPERING

I'll never forget how I papered my first room, and how I got into hanging wallpaper to start with. At the time, I was working in a factory on the night shift and was looking for any escape I could find, even if I had to wind up being a paperhanger. While growing up in a small southern-Indiana town I had seen it done many times, even though I had never tried it myself. Herman Schauberger was sort of the local free-lance paperhanger on evenings and weekends. The rest of the time he worked in a local factory making toilet seats. Mr. Schauberger was the father of one of my best friends, and the two of us used to accompany him down the street to paperhanging jobs, taking turns pushing the wheelbarrow which was loaded with ladders, walking boards, paste table, buckets and such. Mr. Schauberger was a very quiet man, and it's strange to think back and never recall his speaking one word to me in the fifteen-odd years during which we went fishing and did hundreds of other things together besides our several-times-each-week jaunt to some house with the papering equipment. But anyway, Mr. Schauberger finally gave up hanging paper on evenings and weekends, and

To wallpaper, you'll need paste and bucket, a wide-blade knife, scissors, screwdriver, seam roller, razor-blade cutter and extra blades, a rule, a chalk line, paste brush and smoothing brush, plus a long straightedge and a pasting table.

all the equipment was gathering dust underneath his back porch. As I recall, I paid him $15 for the whole outfit including the wheelbarrow. The wheelbarrow was very important because I didn't have a car to haul the stuff from job to job. As luck would have it, my first job took me a couple of miles out of town to paper a living room for the Keisers. I talked another friend into hauling everything out to the house in her car, and I began what was to be a masterful job. I had often watched Mr. Schauberger set up his two ladders, stretch the walking board in between, paste up the paper, then smooth it on the ceiling. So I proceeded accordingly. I took the folded strip of paper on one arm and a smoothing brush in the other hand, and try as I would, the paper came down as fast as I could put it up. After ruining at least a couple of rolls, I finally got the knack of it, and although I'll never win prizes as a wallpaper hanger, I can now do a creditable job with paper, canvas or vinyl.

If you're going to paper a room, first get the proper equipment! You'll find that most of the equipment-rental companies will provide a complete wallpapering outfit for just a few dollars a day. It's worth every penny! My basic papering outfit consists of two ladders, a walking board, one paste bucket, a paste brush, a smoothing brush, a large pair of scissors, a serrated trimming tool, a couple of clean rags, a wooden yardstick and a pasting table with a trimmer knife. A regular pasting table, which you get with the rental equipment, makes all the difference in the world in the ease of getting the job done. One edge of the table has a steel channel into which a knife-type trimmer inserts. This allows you to make straight cuts on long strips of paper. The table is also the right size for precutting and pasting the strips of paper.

Let's assume you have already removed all old loose paper, filled all the cracks and holes with spackle, and sanded them smooth (see preceding chapter for directions on wall repair). One other decision you must make is whether or not to "size" the walls. I always do before I paper. It's well worth the time and trouble, and you don't have to worry about the paper popping loose in a couple of months and the job having to be redone. Buy a package of sizing from the paint or wallpaper store and brush it on with a large paintbrush. The sizing mix will be very watery and easy to apply. Let it dry. Now you're ready to begin.

Start with the ceiling! Most ceiling-type papers have a nondescript pattern, so it is not necessary to try to match the pattern as you apply the paper. If your ceiling paper does have a pronounced pattern, or if you are papering the ceiling with the same pattern as the sidewalls, then refer to the instructions below for matching and cutting sidewall paper. Measure the shorter width of the ceiling, because it is usually easier to handle smaller lengths of paper. Cut each strip at least 4" longer than what you need. Measure the ceiling in its other dimension and decide how many strips will be required to cover the entire area. Now, carefully cut all of the strips needed for the ceiling and place them pattern side down on the paste table.

Let's say you have ten or twelve strips of paper on the table. What you are concerned with now is the top two strips. The very top one should be carefully aligned with the front edge of the table. The second strip should be aligned with the back edge of the table. Do this so that the excess paste will not get on the front of the paper. When you align the two strips properly, the top strip will be adequately pasted on its front edge, and the second strip will catch the excess as you paste the back edge. Now take your paste brush and make sure that every square inch of paper has been endowed with a liberal amount of paste. Usually the strip of paper will be longer than the paste table, so fold over the pasted part of the strip paste side to paste side; then slip the folded part over the end of the table and paste the remaining portion of the strip. Now fold this together also, leaving about a 3" space in between the two folded sections. Drape the strip over your left arm* and climb up onto the walking board. Your head should be about 8" from the ceiling. Unfold half of the strip and with both hands and arms working together, push the pasted surface of the paper against the ceiling.

Your main concern now is the alignment of the paper. The paste will let you slide the strip around enough so you can start it straight. The edge that meets the wall

*This, of course, assumes that you are right-handed. If not, adjust otherwise.

1   2

1 Cut eight or ten strips at one time; then turn the paper or wall covering face side down on the pasting table. Apply a liberal amount of
  paste. To get rid of the lumps, beat the paste with a whisk-type
  beater, or even use an electric mixer.
2 Usually the strip of paper will be longer than the table, so it's advisable to fold the paper over, paste side to paste side, in order to paste
  the remainder of the strip. This fold-over process also keeps the paste
  from drying out and makes the strip of paper easier to handle when
  you get up on a ladder.

must, of course, be butted. Now it's like putting a long strip of cellophane tape on a piece of paper. You have one end sort of stuck to the ceiling. Continue to support the remaining part of the strip with your left arm and hand and then, using the smoothing brush in your right hand, press the brush against the paper and walk along the board as you stick the paper to the ceiling. Take your time, and make sure you have pressed every square inch of the paper against the ceiling as you go along. Usually, at about this time, the end you first pasted to the ceiling comes loose as you walk down the board. If repeated attempts to restick the strip fail, about the only thing you can do is take it down, go back to the paste table and paste it up again.

Right about here, you'll be tempted to call some paperhanger whose advertisement you saw in the paper that morning. Don't do it! You've already learned a lot, and from here on in it will get easier. The first strip on the ceiling is the hardest. Once it is up, each succeeding strip goes on easier, and even butting the edges together seems simple after the first two or three.

Eventually you'll have the ceiling papered, and now you must trim away the excess paper that is probably drooping down on the sidewalls in a variety of places. There are all sorts of tools that can be used for this. Many prefer the serrated wheel, which will trim the paper in a neat line where the ceiling and sidewall join. If you got some paste on the face of the paper, take a damp cloth and wipe it away before it dries.

Now you're ready for the sidewalls. Measure the height of the walls from the ceiling to the baseboard. Allow 3″–4″ extra. Unroll the first strip of sidewall paper, measure and cut. The yardstick is a handy straightedge for tearing off strips. You cannot simply cut all strips of sidewall the same length and have a matched pattern. If the roll of paper has both edges trimmed, you must match the paper as you tear it. You'll soon discover that in matching the pattern you have anywhere from 3″ to 10″ of waste on each piece. This is because the pattern on wallpaper repeats itself every 3″ to 18″. The waste is determined by where you must lop off the bottom of the preceding piece. The only sure way is to carefully match the pattern edges before tearing each strip. Make ten strips, and flop them over on the table, pattern side down, for pasting the same way you did the ceiling strips.

Now you're ready to hang the first strip on the wall. Start at a corner of the room, preferably the darkest corner or the one behind a door. The first strip must be perfectly vertical. Do **not** line the paper up with the corner, because the room has probably settled just enough to throw the whole wall slightly out of square. If you have a level, use it to find the true vertical line on the wall. If you don't have a level, tie a weight on about a 6′ length of string to serve as a plumb bob. Drive a small finishing nail into the wall, leaving about ½″ of the nail protruding. Then tie the string around the nail, with the weight suspended. When the motion of the weight stops, press the string against the wall and trace a line along the string with a pencil. This will be true vertical. Now hang the first strip of paper so that the edge of the paper corresponds with this true vertical line. You'll find that the corner of the room may be off as much as 1″. Let it be, because it's better to have one corner a little cockeyed than have the entire room listing at a precarious angle. Take the first strip of paper and start hanging from the top of the wall. Using your big, wide smoothing brush, press the paper firmly to the wall and then work right down the strip to the baseboard. I always have excess paper at both the top and bottom,

1   2

1 Begin papering the sidewall in a corner. Measure out from the corner
  the width of the paper and use a plumb bob to establish a true vertical line. Mark that line on the wall so that the first strip of paper
  will be perfectly plumb.
2 Start hanging the paper where the wall meets the ceiling. As in this
  picture, the first strip should have the left edge of the paper halfway
  through the corner and the right edge following the line drawn on
  the wall.

1 Use your smoothing brush to press the paper against the wall. Brush out any air bubbles that you see.

2 Brush the paper tight against the wall right down to the baseboard. Next, use your wide-blade knife as a guide for cutting the excess paper. Hold the knife tight against the wall and baseboard, then run the razor-blade knife along the wide knife for a perfect trim.

which I trim before starting on the next strip. When you come to the next corner, do it exactly like the other strips except that you must work the paper tightly into the corner itself. Then take a serrated cutter or a razor-blade knife and carefully slit down the corner for the entire length of the paper. Again take your brush, and work the paper well into the corner. Now, using your level or plumb bob, make sure that the remainder of the strip, which has turned the corner and is now on the next wall, follows a true vertical line. If you simply go around the corner without cutting the paper, you'll eventually be sorry. Many amateur paperhangers try this, to their disappointment.

Windows and doors offer no real complications if you'll just use a little common sense. For example, say you have 6″ of blank wall between your last strip and a door or window frame. Put the paper up the same way you would if the door or window was not there. After pressing the paper well against the wall with your brush, carefully cut the paper with your knife along the edge of the doorframe and throw the waste piece away. The same technique applies to papering around bookshelves or any other built-in furniture in the room.

While the paste is still wet, roll down each seam in the paper with a small 25-cent tool called a seamer. This is little more than a handle with an elongated wooden wheel on one end. It will ensure that the paper will not bulge loose at the seams, and also bring any excess paste to the surface of the paper. Also, keep a big flat sponge in clean water handy so you can wipe excess paste from the face of the paper before it dries. Roll down the seam with the roller, then wipe with the sponge.

Wallpaper borders use to be the vogue, but you seldom see them anymore. I prefer using a piece of crown molding where the ceiling meets the wall. Painted or stained to complement the colors of the wallpaper, it makes for a much more professional-looking job. There are all kinds of moldings available at lumberyards or at the big hardware department stores. The only skill required for installation is cutting the molding at an angle in the corners. A small, inexpensive miter box can solve that problem for you. You can also use one of the new adhesives to glue the molding in place rather than nail it up. Ask your hardware dealer for an appropriate one. I would also suggest that if you use the molding idea, you paint or stain the molding before you put it in place. It's easier to work with on the floor or a table—and besides, you won't mess up your fresh, new wallpaper job.

For the average wallpapering job you will need the following tools:

Two 6′ ladders ⎫ for ceilings; one ladder if you're
Walk board ⎭ doing only walls
Pasting and trimming table
Wooden or metal yardstick
Paste brush
Smoothing brush
Sponge or old rags
Razor-blade knife or serrated cutter
Pair of scissors
Seam roller
Paste bucket
Wheat paste
Wallpaper
Plumb bob or spirit level

There are a variety of papers on the market. All of them are installed pretty much the same way, from old-fashioned cheap paper to the new vinyls. I have used prepasted paper, but still prefer the sloppy way for a couple of reasons. I found the prepasted paper I used to be more prone to coming unfastened, because it rarely has enough paste on it. And secondly, I found it messier to soak the prepasted paper than it is to paste.

Directions on how to mix wallpaper paste are printed on the package. It's just mixing with water. Follow the directions **carefully.** The paste will have a tendency to be lumpy, so it's wise to have a piece of cheesecloth to strain the paste before putting it on the paper. Don't worry about the bubbles that may appear as the paper goes up on the wall. Ninety-nine percent of them will disappear when the paste dries.

I still believe the hardest job about wallpapering is deciding on the pattern. Natalie spends hours going through wallpaper books and taking swatches of upholstery material to stores. Frankly, you can paper a room in half the time it takes your wife to make up her mind which paper to use.

Vinyl wall covering has many advantages. First, since it is a plastic-type material, it is very washable. Second, if you get tired of the pattern, you can pull each strip off the wall almost as easily as you put it up! If you use the regular paper, have it plastic-coated by the dealer before you hang it. The thin coat of plastic will increase the paper's life several times, and although not as thoroughly washable as the pure vinyl, it is moderately washable and much more serviceable. Don't worry about any change in appearance because of the coating. You won't be able to tell the difference, and the paper will not appear shiny.

In my experience, the extra-wide vinyls are hardest to hang, particularly on ceilings. If you have never tried it, may I suggest not using the extra-wide rolls for your first job. The most important thing is convincing yourself you can do it before you start. Take your time, and don't argue with each other while you're doing it. According to my statistics, more divorces start over hanging wallpaper than any other cause. (I always lock Natalie in a closet until the job's done.)

Natalie's Notes

Most of the do-it-yourself wallpaper hangers I know are women, and many of them are better than some professionals I've had working for me. I think when it comes to home decoration, women are more particular than men (Wally says "fussy") and have more patience, which is a necessity when you're hanging paper. If you make a mistake, just do it over—which is why I usually buy an extra roll of paper. After having advised my husband (Wally says "nagged") these past four years, I've turned him into a pretty fair wallpaper hanger. I still won't let him pick out the paper, however.

3 PANELING

Since this is supposed to be a book about how "simple" a lot of tasks can be, I hesitate to tell you about the time Natalie and I spent three months installing wood paneling in one room! In addition to the two of us, we even had a carpenter and his wife doing most of the work. It was a rather exceptional undertaking because we were using antique paneling which had previously been used to decorate the president's office of the Black, Starr, Frost and Gorham silver company in New York City. The building in which the company was located was demolished, and we ended up with the paneling. Each section of paneling had to be dismantled, reduced in size to fit our 10′ ceilings and remitered. The result was something less than sensational, but worth every hour of work.

That kind of paneling job is far from simple, but you're not likely to face it. There now is paneling available that is easier to install than hanging wallpaper! I am constantly amazed at the varieties offered and the wide price range, depending on your choice of wood or finish. Prices begin on very cheap paneling at around $3 for a damaged or discontinued 4′ x 8′ piece and range as high as $100 or

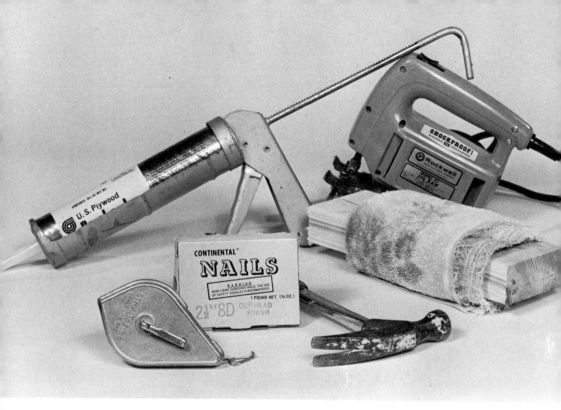

Tools for paneling include caulk gun and adhesive, electric jigsaw, cloth-covered block of wood, chalk line, nails, hammer and scribe.

even more. But here, as well as in other remodeling jobs, the price of installation often exceeds material costs, and if you do the job yourself you can invest in a better-grade paneling and have a much nicer-looking room or home.

The easiest kind of installation is on a nice, flat wall with no windows or doors. On that type of wall you can glue the paneling in place in an hour or so and transform the entire room. Going around doors and windows will take a little longer and you'll need some special tools, but you can do it if you follow my directions and use a little common sense.

I have never seen a house that was perfectly square, and I am going to assume that your home is no exception. Even as a house is being built it begins to settle fractions of an inch, and since the corners do not all settle the same fraction of an inch, you will have a deviation from "square," however slight. The 4′ x 8′ panels are square, and therein lies the problem. First, remove the old baseboard and other trim. You will want to start paneling in one of the corners of the room, and when you try the first section of paneling in the corner, you must make sure the panel will be absolutely vertical. You can use a carpenter's level, a chalk line or a plumb bob. For a plumb bob, take a 6′ length of string and tie a weight on one end. Make a loop in the other end of the string and tack a nail in the wall. Put the loop over the nail, and when the string stops swinging, it will rest in a true vertical line.

Push the first section of paneling firmly into the corner, and then mark a line along the edge of the panel that is not in the corner. Take the first panel down and check the line to make sure it is vertical. If it is "off," you must trim the edge of the panel that fits against the corner. You can saw it, plane it or sand it, depending on how much wood you have to remove. Another way you can determine how much to cut off the first panel is by using a compass or scribe. Do it this way. Set the panel into the corner, bottom edge resting on the floor, and hold it flat against the wall. Use the plumb bob to make sure that it is vertical. If the panel touches tight against one part of the corner and gaps away from the corner at another place, this will show you how much you must trim that panel. The gap will be at either the top or the bottom. Usually, the panel will fit tight against the corner at the bottom and gap away from it at the top. Measure the width of the gap and set your compass or scribe to that measurement. For example, ½″. Still holding the panel against the wall, put one leg of the scribe or compass in the corner and let the other leg extend onto the panel. Now, draw the compass or scribe from top to bottom of the panel, leaving either a pencil mark or a scratch on the face of the panel. Remove

 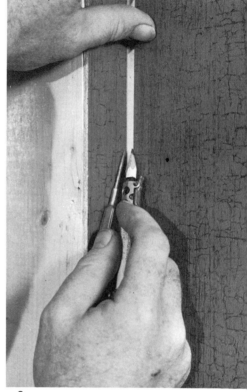

1   2

1 Start in a corner and test the first sheet of paneling to determine the "plumb" of the wall. Most corners like this one will be at least ¼" "off." The first sheet of paneling must be installed perfectly vertical. Use either a plumb bob or a level, make a mark and align the sheet of paneling with that mark. Next check the corner, because the panel will have to be trimmed to fit.

2 Using a scribe, find the widest gap between the corner and the sheet of paneling. Adjust the scribe to this measurement, as I am doing here.

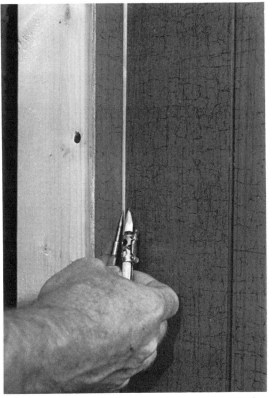 

1   2

1 Draw the scribe down the corner, one leg into the corner of the wall,
  the other leg marking the face of the panel. Remove the sliver of
  paneling so marked and you have compensated for the out-of-plumb
  wall.
2 Here's a tip to remember! When cutting paneling with an electric
  saw, cut, if possible, from the back of the panel. This keeps the saw
  itself from scratching the face of the panel.

the panel and cut along the line left by the scribe. Now you're ready to start installation.

If you're paneling an existing wall in your home, the panels can be installed over any dry, tight surface. Neither paint nor wallpaper has to be removed as long as the paint isn't flaking or the wallpaper isn't loose. I prefer using a panel adhesive rather than nails. For the amateur, it's difficult to find the upright studs in the wall to nail into, and with adhesive you won't have to worry about it. Buy a "caulk gun" from the paneling dealer, and he'll recommend how many tubes of adhesive you'll need to do your particular job. You apply the adhesive to the wall in a "bead," by putting the nozzle of the adhesive tube against the surface of the wall, squeezing the handle of the gun and squirting the gooey stuff onto the wall in a ½″-wide string. Put a bead of the adhesive horizontally across the top and bottom of the space for the first panel, down about 2″ from the ceiling and up about 2″ from the floor. Now, put a bead of adhesive in two vertical lines, each in about 2″ from where the edges of the panel will fit. Run two more beads of adhesive vertically down the middle of the area.

Take the 4′ x 8′ sheet of paneling and press it firmly against the wall so that it makes good contact with the adhesive. Make sure it fits into the corner in a neat fashion and that all parts of the panel are tight against the wall. Drive in a couple of finishing nails at the top to hold the panel in place.

Pull the bottom of the panel out from the wall about 3″–4″ to allow the adhesive to become tacky. The adhesive will look like bubble gum at this point if you look in the crack between the panel and the wall. Let the air circulate behind the panel for seven or eight minutes; then push the panel back up against the wall and, using a cloth-covered block and a hammer, gently tap the block to re-

1

2

3

1 Using a caulk gun, apply the adhesive to the wall or studs. I prefer using a sort of dotted-line effect. Don't worry about the panel coming loose; the adhesive holds even better than nails.
2 Take the panel and move it into place.
3 Position the panel so that it is perfectly vertical; then use a couple of small finishing nails to hold the top of the panel in place.

1 Next, press the panel against the adhesive-coated wall so that the adhesive is transferred to the panel.

2 Now, pull the panel away from the wall where the panel meets the floor. The two finishing nails will hold the panel at the top. Let air circulate behind the panel for six to eight minutes so that the adhesive can set.

3 After six to eight minutes, press the panel firmly against the wall, and using a cloth-covered block of wood and a hammer, gently tap the face of the panel for the best adhesion.

1

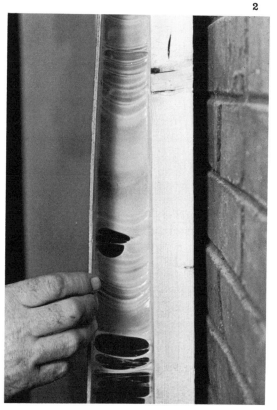

2

3

move all air pockets and to make sure the panel fits tightly against the wall. Since you have already determined that the first panel is vertical, the rest will automatically be as you butt panel after panel to the preceding one. Each corner must be checked the same as the first one, but the panels in between don't have to be.

If the wall doesn't have either doors or windows, the only cutting you have to do is enough to square the corners, and perhaps to cut one section of the paneling unless the wall width is divisible by four (8′ wide, 12′ wide, 16′, etc.). But where doors and windows are involved, and electrical wall outlets, etc., you're going to have to learn to cut and notch paneling before you can complete the job. The easiest way to go around windows and doors is to first remove the old woodwork. Quite often in a remodeling job you will want to replace that woodwork anyway with new molding that matches the panels. You can buy the new molding from your panel supplier, already prefinished for an exact match. But save that old woodwork if you prefer—and if you're going to save it, then you have to use care in removing it. Use a pry bar or a heavy screwdriver to pry the old molding out from the wall. Once it starts to come loose, each piece will come off in one section. (You'll usually have four sections per window, three sections per door.) On electrical outlets you must remove the face plate before the panel goes onto the wall, and to do this you'll find one screw in the center of the plate which holds it together.

My brother-in-law is in the furniture business, and his company makes some of the finest furniture in the world. It is his claim that anytime you work with wood you have a ¼″ tolerance. Keep that in mind as you start trimming and cutting the panels to fit around the doors and windows. Another rule to remember is "Measure twice and cut once"—one more way to keep from making the wrong cut in your paneling.

There is no way to wave a magic wand to make cutting around doors and windows a snap. The most important tool to use is your head. Panel as close to the window or door as the last 4′ section allows. Depending on where the door or window may be, the last section of paneling may be inches from the opening or several feet. Let's say the last full panel you installed on the wall is 2′ away from a doorframe. Measure the height of the door, not inside the frame, but to a point where the panel will fit over the top of the door. Let's say that measurement is 6′9″. Since the sections of paneling are 4′ wide, and the last panel on the wall is 2′ from the door, you don't have to be a mathematical genius to figure out that the next section of paneling you install will have to have a couple of feet trimmed away where the panel extends into the doorway itself. Put the panel on a couple of sawhorses, the floor or a table—wherever you're working—and first measure the height of the door along the edge of the panel that has to be cut. Do the same with the other edge, but mark the other edge carefully so that the mark will not show after the panel has been installed. Using a straightedge, lightly trace a line from one mark to the other on the **back** of the panel. Determine again which edge you are going to cut off, and measure 2′ along the lightly traced line and make a mark. Go to the bottom of the panel, and again measure 2′ from the edge that will be cut off and make a mark. Now, draw a vertical line down the panel connecting the last two marks that you made. The lines will now represent the area to be sawed.

You can cut the paneling with a handsaw, a saber saw or any sort of power saw; but make sure that the saw blade has fine teeth, because the paneling is fragile to a point, and remember that it doesn't need a heavy hand, because it is only ¼″ thick.

The same procedure will work in going around a window, etc. Don't forget to measure twice and cut once, and once you try measuring twice you'll be amazed how many times you would have made an error if you hadn't double-checked yourself.

Electrical outlets already in the wall are the most disgusting things to go around. Here again you have to rely on measuring and then precutting the panel before it goes up. But here again the ¼″ tolerance comes in handy, and if you take your time, measure carefully and follow instructions, there is absolutely no reason why you can't "do-it-yourself."

After all the panels have been installed and you're patting yourself on the back, you may want to consider adding some moldings to enhance the overall appearance. I'm a sucker for crown molding, the molding that attaches where the wall joins the ceiling. Again, you can buy this in several different styles and sizes, depending on your taste. Or if your local hardware or home-supply store doesn't have what you want, you can always journey to a lumberyard and pick out something from a wider variety. You'll have to match the finish to the panels, but it can be done with a little experimentation and the aid of color guides the large manufacturers put out. Moldings are also available to fit into the corners, just in case you measured wrong and you have a ½″ gap where you shouldn't. You can also buy moldings for outside corners, window and door moldings, baseboard and even kits that will convert doors to harmonize better with the rest of the room. The free booklets put out by most paneling manufacturers do tend to oversimplify just a bit the ease with which paneling can be installed, but they are also chock-full of good information and should be digested accordingly.

Something not too many people know is that paneling can be removed even easier than it can be installed. If you put it up with adhesive, you can simply pull it off the wall with a little muscle. I mention this because maybe you paneled a home years ago and because of budget didn't get the kind of paneling you would really like to have bought. Why not change it? As you pull off each old panel, you have a ready-made pattern for cutting the new one. You may pull some of the plaster off the wall when you take the old paneling down, but not enough to hurt anything or to cause the house to collapse. I particularly like wood walls—and not just because I do paneling commercials on television. Sometimes one wall of paneling is all you need to properly accent a room; other rooms may lend themselves to total paneling. But remember, in your home you can have anything you like if you can afford it—sooo, decide what you want and do it, because you can do it if you try!

Natalie's Notes

To give you an idea of how popular installing your own paneling has become, our friends at U.S. Plywood recently told us that 75 percent of the paneling they make is sold to do-it-yourselfers.

We recently paneled the third floor of our home, which we use as our office. We selected walnut paneling, which we complemented with carpeting in rich red and gold tones. In spite of the fact that it is still our office, it has become one of the warmest and most inviting rooms in our house. It's amazing how pleasant surroundings can make balancing a checkbook bearable.

The price range as well as the variety of different woods and colors available makes paneling such a popular way of hiding boring or unsightly walls.

4 ARTIFICIAL STONE AND BRICK

I'm really not too big on using simulated products in place of the real thing, but on occasion the real thing is just beyond the realm of common sense and you have to compromise somehow, some way.

For example, if you've been longing for a brick wall in your kitchen, or an extra fireplace in some other room of your home, it's darn near impossible to use real brick without spending a fortune. It isn't that real bricks cost so much, but in order to support their tremendous weight you must have a substantial footing that will bear the weight. More often than not it isn't practical to make such an installation, and if you are planning either a brick wall or a fireplace in a second-floor bedroom, it is impossible! It's in places like these that I would recommend artificial brick or stone.

Usually the artificial products cost as much as the real thing, and sometimes more! You will make your savings by doing the job yourself, and invariably installation is easier when you use artificial products. There are dozens of different kinds of artificial brick, for example. You can buy a brick-patterned wallpaper, or a thin plastic sheet of simulated bricks that has its own sticky backing, or you can buy an artificial brick which you install brick by brick in an adhesive. There are probably other types in addition to the ones I've mentioned. The brick wallpaper won't fool anyone who looks at it. The plastic-sheet stuff may look like the real thing at first glance, but one touch and you know it's fake. The artificial bricks, usually a cast product colored to look like brick and installed a brick at a time, will come within an edge of looking like the real McCoy. The cast bricks are also harder to install, so you will have to make a decision as to whether the effect is worth the extra money and effort.

The brick wallpaper goes up just like any wallpaper, and you can refer to that chapter for installation procedures. The plastic-sheet material comes in a variety of sizes, patterns and colors. Some of it simulates stone in a variety of colors, while other patterns include yellow or red brick in a variety of styles. The plastic material is very thin and brittle, and usually comes with a peel-off backing so that it will adhere to any clean surface. The sections are approximately 1' x 4', and interlock so that the effect of the pattern is unbroken. I wouldn't think that this type of material should be used in an area where it could encounter a lot of contact or wear. It seems rather fragile and certainly could not be described as childproof. For the apartment dweller, it might be the perfect answer to a temporary decorating problem.

If you want a brick wall that will be substantially permanent, can take a considerable amount of abuse and will look almost as good as the real thing, you should use the brick-by-brick method. This material gives you almost all the advantages of a real brick wall without the weight of real bricks. The "bricks" are actually a "slice" of bricklike material which is about ½" thick. The face of the slice of brick conforms almost exactly to the real thing, and even when you run your hand across the surface it is difficult to discern the difference. The bricklike material comes pre-cut and packaged and ready for use. Each manufacturer has his own idea about installation, and it ranges from a combination adhesive grout to using a caulk gun for the grout. The combination adhesive grout eliminates a second step and I'll explain it first.

The adhesive comes premixed in one-gallon and five-gallon containers. It is first applied to any clean surface with a broad putty knife or trowel, and the bricks are then pressed into place by hand. The adhesive dries very quickly, and at least one manufacturer recommends that you start at the top of the wall and work your way down. The adhesive is applied to the wall in a thick layer—3/16″ to ¼″ or manufacturer's recommendation—because when you press the brick in place, the excess you squeeze out becomes the mortar joint between the brick pieces. The adhesive usually comes in three colors: white, gray and black.

When you start your installation, make sure the first row of bricks that you install on the wall follows a straight line. You can use a carpenter's level to determine this. Place the level against the wall horizontally, center the little bubble in the middle of the level, then draw a pencil line on the wall.

The adhesive that I have used gives you about fifteen minutes' work time before it starts to harden. Which means, don't spread adhesive on too much of the wall or it will dry out before you are able to apply the bricks. Work about two rows at a time. Apply the thick adhesive, press the first row into place, then continue on to the second row. Then apply enough adhesive for the next two rows and repeat the process. The only other trick to installing this type of brick is maintaining the same distance between bricks. You can fashion a gauge out of a scrap of wood which will serve the purpose. Brick mortar joints (the spaces between the bricks) are usually from ¼" to ½" wide. Cut a piece of wood to the size you want the joint and periodically check the distance between the pieces of brick.

There are all sorts of patterns you can use in installing the brick. The standard running bond means bricks installed lengthwise in each row with every other row staggered. Common bond means the same as running bond except that every sixth row of bricks you use the end dimension of the brick as the face (not possible with simulated bricks without cutting the bricklike material). For a more modern effect, I would suggest stacked bricks, which means each row of bricks is exactly in line with every other row. This effect gives you strong vertical lines and will tend to add height to a room. Artificial brick can be cut by conventional stone-cutting methods—an electric saw with a stone blade, a hacksaw, etc.

A manufacturing plant on Cape Cod makes artificial stone and brick from a plastic resin that is as close to the real thing as any I've seen. The company recommends applying the material on an already applied adhesive; pressing the bricks into place; then, by using an ordinary caulk gun, running the mortar into the cracks. This method has one big advantage over applying a thick adhesive: it costs less! But anytime you start looking for a product to simulate the real thing, it isn't going to be cheap. Both materials I've described will cost as much as the real thing. Your savings will be in providing the labor free, and possibly being able to install an artificial brick or stone wall where a real one could not be installed.

A number of years ago, and perhaps still today, a fiber-

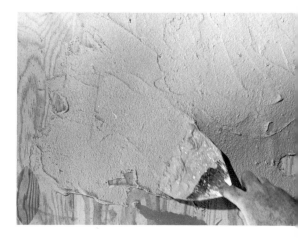

First spread mortar on the area where the stone or brick is to be applied. I use a wide-blade knife, and the manufacturer's directions usually call for a layer of mortar at least ¼″ thick (check the package). It's a messy job, so be sure to protect the floor.

The mortar is also an adhesive. Simply press the brick on and hold for about ten or fifteen seconds, and it will stay in place.

The thickness of the mortar will determine the look of the finished job. Here the mortar is oozing around the brick and if not wiped off, will harden as the kind of mortar joint you see here.

glass stone was on the market which could be used inside or outside. The fiber-glass stone also came in sheets approximately 1' x 4', and was really indistinguishable from the real stone. It came in both a white limestone and a yellow sandstone pattern and was particularly adaptable for the outside wall of porches, foundation walls and planters. This material could be nailed onto any surface; then, using a caulk gun, you filled the mortar joints and concealed the nails. You could cut the material with a regular handsaw. Its primary drawback, as I recall, was its expense.

Before any of these products were available, I once made my own brick wall in the kitchen of a house by using insulating brick siding. In the Midwest, they used to install this stuff on innumerable houses. It is designed for exteriors and is available in a variety of colors and patterns. It looks pretty good when you use it on the inside of a house, but it does tend to shed! Little grainy particles will drop off every day until the kitchen will look like it has a bad case of dandruff. Its greatest advantage is that it's cheap. I would never recommend it to anyone, but it's simple to install if you want to. You can apply it with nails over any kind of surface, and if you're planning on selling the house, you won't have to sweep up the granules every morning. Walking into a kitchen with that stuff on the walls is like walking across the beach!

What I'm really trying to say is: don't be afraid to use a little ingenuity. Go into a building-supply dealer's and look over the products that are available. You might find a brand-new way to use an old reliable product and save yourself a lot of money. I don't really believe that everyone wants a home exactly like someone else's. The only way you can make yours different is to find a new way to use products that are available. Remember, too, that sometimes a brick wall is more effective if it isn't all brick. You can cut a slice from an old beam and install it among the bricks. The end of the beam will look like the end of an old beam! The same adhesive will hold wood in place as well as brick or stone. You can also combine brick and stone for an unusual effect. In fact, when you use the artificial stuff, the more novel you become the better it looks, because rather than being compared with a regular brick or stone wall, it will be valued for its unusual and decorative appearance.

Natalie's Notes

The only time I ever used any of the artificial products Wally mentions was when I was in charge of scenery for a grade-school play and used the plastic brick for a fake fireplace. And to be brutally frank, I intend for that to be my one and only experience with ersatz brick—or stone, for that matter. Unfortunately, however, circumstances often dictate taste, and I must admit I would resort to using simulated brick for an upstairs fireplace rather than have the floor cave in.

5 BEAMED CEILINGS

If you really like beamed ceilings, there is no reason in the world why you can't have them! I know it looks complicated, but beaming ceilings can be as simple or as exasperating as you would like to make it. I suppose the purist would like to have the original hand-hewn beams from an old barn to install in the kitchen or living room or wherever. You can do it that way, and the results are worth the effort.

But using the old original beams will give you a number of problems that you will not encounter using some new products that are now available. For example, most of the old barn beams that you will find are solid oak. They were made out of oak because it was one of the strongest woods the builders could use, but it is also one of the heaviest. An 8″ x 8″ oak beam may not weigh a ton, but you'll think it does when you lift it to a ceiling! The most difficult thing about using old oak beams is finding a satisfactory way to hold them in place. If you're beaming an existing room in your house, you're not looking for a beam for strength. The only real purpose the beam will serve is decoration, so why use something as heavy as oak? You

If you want the hand-hewn look, you can do that too. Using the 2"-wide chisel, dig into the beam and remove small chunks of wood. It works very well, and after the staining or whatever, you'll think Abe Lincoln worked the beam over.

can buy pine or fir or hemlock beams, which will serve the purpose. If you want a rustic hand-hewn look, you can rough them up with a hammer and chisel or with a hatchet. (We preferred a more finished look for the beams that I installed in the kitchen of our home, so I didn't bother to rough them up. Instead, I routed the edges of the 4" x 6" beams.) Also, if you use a softwood beam instead of oak, you'll find staining it more satisfactory, because the softer woods take stain better than hardwoods.

I suppose the ideal arrangement is to find old barn beams that were hewn out of a pine log. They would show age, ax marks and all the other "goodies" that are desirable in beams for ceilings.

But there are new products available that do indeed look authentic once they are installed. The simplest way to beam is to use the new plastic products available at most good lumberyards. They are artificial beams, made of foamed polyurethane, already finished and in several styles. You can get a hand-hewn Early American look in beams 8" x 8" that weigh only a few ounces per foot. I have also seen them in French Provincial and Modern styling in a variety of sizes. This type of beam is easy to cut, goes up with an adhesive instead of nails and looks great once it's in place. The only drawback is the price. This type of beam is expensive, sometimes costing as much as $3 or $4 per foot.

You can also buy prefabricated beams made out of plywood. They are already machined to give a hand-hewn look and are relatively easy to assemble and put in place.

I must admit that I prefer the real thing to something phony, even if you can't tell the difference once it is in place. When I beamed the kitchen ceiling in our home I used hemlock beams and was thoroughly satisfied with the result. The next time I do a beaming job, I'll probably use old barn beams if I can figure out a way to hold them up.

Let me explain and show you by illustration one way you can install a new ceiling and beam it at the same time for a relatively small amount of money. Older homes lend themselves to a beaming job more than the newer ones (in my opinion), and I'll assume that you're the proud possessor of an older house.

Before I started beaming our kitchen ceiling, it was really a mess. Plaster was missing, lath was showing through and the upstairs bathroom sprayed water every time someone flushed the toilet. Natalie used to wear a raincoat to make coffee, and threatened to buy a hard hat after being clobbered with falling plaster. Of course, the leak in the bathroom had to be repaired first, and after that was done we turned our efforts to repairing the ceiling.

The ceiling in the kitchen was 9′6″ in height, which gave us a considerable amount of leeway in working out a solution. I decided early to forget about repairing the original ceiling and instead to drop down about 12″ and install a new ceiling.

The previous owner of the house had left a number of hemlock beams in the barn, and since the cheapest way to get material is for free, I decided to use what I had. The beams were 4″ x 6″ and up to 12′ in length.

It was necessary to use real beams because the beams themselves were going to support the new ceiling I had in mind. First I put perimeter beams around the room and attached them to the wall studs with heavy nails. The room itself was 12′ x 12′, which necessitated notching the perimeter beams every 4′ so I could drop in crossbeams.

Notching beams is not at all complicated as long as you measure correctly. The physical part of removing the hunk of wood from the notch is easily accomplished with a saw, wide wood chisel and hammer. Once the perimeter beams were installed, and the nails carefully countersunk so they wouldn't show, I notched the ends of the beams that were to be installed in a lattice fashion spanning the room.

For ease of installation, I used two 12′ beams, notching each end to fit into the notches in the perimeter beams, and also cutting notches at 4′ intervals so that other beams could intersect. The 12′ lengths dropped right into place, and no nails or fasteners were required.

Next, I cut six pieces of beam each 4′ in length and notched the ends of each one, and these too went together like pieces of a jigsaw puzzle. At this point, the beams not only were self-supporting but in fact could support the additional ceiling materials required. The ceiling now looked like a lattice of beams, with the beams installed 4′ on center across the area.

To fill in the empty spaces I decided to use ¼″ plywood covered with wallpaper. Since plywood is available in 4′ x 8′ sheets, it was a simple job for the lumberyard to supply

1 The only place you have to secure a suspended ceiling like this is at the walls. If you get a little sag in the middle of the ceiling because of the weight of the beams, you can always attach large screw eyes and turnbuckles from the beams to the old ceiling.

2 Notching the beams is easy. For an interlocking-beam ceiling, first measure the width of the beam that interlocks. Then make a saw cut along the measured line halfway through each section to be joined.

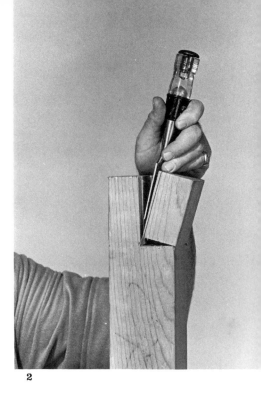

1

2

3

1 Use a 2"-wide wood chisel and hammer to remove the unwanted chunk of wood. First, score the wood lightly with chisel along the measured line.

2 Next, hit the chisel a good hard lick with the hammer and the section will split away from the main part of the beam.

3 After the piece has been removed, dress the area by using the chisel blade as a plane. You'll want the cutout area dressed flat so that it will fit perfectly into the other beam section.

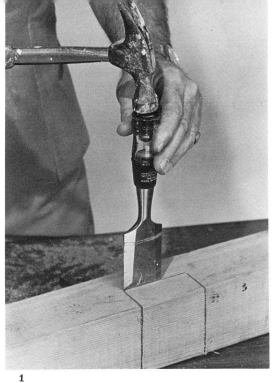

1

2

3

1 For a notch in the middle of a beam you'll have to make two saw cuts, as shown. Next, use the chisel to score along the line. At this point, don't try to knock out the unwanted section of wood. Score about ¼″ deep and this will give you a nice straight edge once the piece is removed.

2 After scoring both sides of the beam, hit the chisel another good lick with the hammer and then pry the section out of the beam.

3 Dress the cut with the chisel until the two pieces interlock perfectly.

1 How about that? You won't even need nails to hold this combination together. See how important it is to make saw cuts nice and straight?

2 Installing the ceiling this way does not require any exposed nails. Notice how one beam interlocks with the others.

me with nine pieces of plywood 4′ x 4′. Before applying the wallpaper to the plywood, I gave the plywood a coat of shellac to seal the wood, let it dry and then pasted the wallpaper on the plywood before I installed the sections in the ceiling. The wallpapered sections of plywood fitted on top of the beams, and when all pieces had been put in place, the result was really sensational!

The only problem I hadn't counted on was the sag in the ceiling toward the middle of the room. This was easily remedied by the use of screw eyes and turnbuckles. I secured two screw eyes in the old ceiling, two more in the 12′ beams at the center of the room. I then ran piano-type wire from screw eye to turnbuckle to screw eye and repeated the process with the other set. Then, by adjusting the turnbuckles I was able to lift the center portion of the ceiling just enough to eliminate the sag.

I later fashioned a chandelier from a buggy doubletree, and using old Tiffany-type stained-glass shades, I had a light fixture that complemented the ceiling perfectly. The total cost for our new ceiling was well under $100 even if I had had to buy the beams! Besides, it was a lot of fun designing the ceiling, picking out the wallpaper and seeing the end result. The old ceiling? I left it just the way it was, falling plaster and all.

Just recently I persuaded a neighbor of mine to use the same beaming technique in a basement recreation room. He used two-by-fours for the beams, and it turned out just great. In fact, the kids papered each plywood panel with a different-patterned wallpaper, and he mounted flush-type ceiling lights into several of the panels, which gave plenty of illumination. This type of ceiling lends itself very well to basements because it is easy to drop this ceiling just a few inches so you can hide exposed pipes and plumbing. You can then paint the beams or stain them, make them

1

2

1 The final step is cutting pieces of ½" plywood to fill in the spaces between the beams. I make a ceiling like this one so that the empty spaces are 4′ x 4′. That way, one sheet of plywood, cut in half, will fill two spaces. You can cover the plywood with a variety of products, but for this I use wallpaper, usually a small Early American–type print. First coat the plywood with shellac, let it dry, then paper the plywood before you put it in place. This is a great ceiling for a kitchen, because you can always remove the plywood panels for cleaning or redecoration.

2 The plywood panels do not have to be nailed to the beams. They will rest on the top of the beams and give the impression of a regular ceiling. If you prefer indirect lighting, you could use translucent plastic panels instead of plywood, or you can even use paneling on the ceiling that matches the walls. This is fun to do because it looks so great when you finish!

modern or primitive, and in cost it's about as inexpensive as any ceiling can be.

Natalie's Notes

I don't think I have ever been more surprised or delighted than I was with the kitchen ceiling that Wally designed and built.

When it was completed, none of our friends who hadn't been around during construction could tell that the ceiling wasn't plaster but, in fact, consisted of six individual sheets of papered plywood.

We chose an Early American print of small flowers, and it complemented beautifully the decor of our kitchen. Another attractive feature of the plywood boards is the fact that you can easily change the wallpaper or even paint the panels whenever you desire. And when spring cleaning time rolls around, think how much easier it is to clean a removable ceiling!

Wally definitely gets an A+ for this ingenious innovation.

6 ROOM DIVIDERS

Once again, this is a subject that can be as varied and interesting as you are creative. There are relatively simple ways to construct room dividers and have them look like something special, and that's what I'll describe here.

For years I have been fascinated by the variety of wood turnings that are now available at super hardware stores and lumberyards. When I was a kid growing up in southern Indiana, we used to call wood turnings like that "porch posts," because every house on the street had a porch, and most of the porch roofs were supported by round wooden posts, turned on a lathe at one of the local factories. Today they are still in vogue, not so much as porch posts as for interior use such as in room dividers.

As I mentioned, I have seen these products for years, but I have never seen any material put out by the manufacturer showing you what you can do with them! A couple of months ago I finally sat down on a box in the lumberyard, and stared intently at the turnings and came up with an idea to make a room divider out of them.

Now, they're not cheap! Wood turnings about 3″ in diameter and 5′ long are approximately $6 apiece, and in the room divider I designed I used ten of them. The turnings are available in almost every length and diameter imaginable, from 3″ long to 12′. Diameter is in proportion to their length, and in almost all cases the wood used is pine or fir. I mention the kind of wood used only because a soft wood such as pine or fir is easier for the amateur to work with. Not only is it easier to sand, nail and drill softer woods, but they will take stains more readily when you're ready to finish the piece. Some of the harder woods like maple are difficult to stain because the pores of the wood are so tight that most stains will not penetrate. That's why commercial furniture makers usually give the hard woods a base coat of absorbent material, then stain the base coat instead of the wood, or let the base coat be the prime coat and apply a pigmented finish over that. This final finish is almost invariably lacquer.

But you will find that pine turnings will easily take almost any kind of stain, and even though the wood grain of pine is not as desirable as that of the hard woods, the strong pine grain is not so noticeable in a turning.

The kind of wood turning you buy for a room divider is determined by the present decor of your home. The larger turnings are available in at least a half dozen different styles, and the ones I have seen include Early American, Mediterranean, French Provincial and Modern. The size turning you buy depends on the height of your ceiling and whether or not you use a solid base such as a bookcase. But let me explain how I put one together. Whether or not you want to make an exact duplicate is beside the point. Perhaps my germ of an idea will sprout something else in your mind.

I bought ten of the turnings, each 5′ long and approximately 2½″ in diameter. I picked an Early American style. I made my room divider for a room with an 8′ ceiling. Let's assume you want a divider so you can convert a corner of a room into a private nook. Maybe you want a sewing corner or an area for a small desk with a telephone, but find such an arrangement is not possible without some sort of divider or partition. O.K. I designed my divider so it would extend out from the wall a distance of 4'. The divider itself was a base bookcase 3' up from the floor. In my case, I made the bookcase. However, you can also buy a new unfinished bookcase to use for this purpose, and the new ones available are almost always made of pine, which means you'll have no problems staining the turnings and bookcase to match.

The 3'-high base does not necessarily have to be anything but a support, and if you have a paneled room where you're adding this type of divider you might also want to panel the base so it will match the rest of the room. Any way you do it is fine as long as you're happy with the finished job.

Since the length of the wood turnings is predetermined, you have to adjust the size of the base so the turnings will fill the gap between the top of the base and the ceiling. Don't assume your room has an 8' ceiling without measuring it. Quite often an 8' ceiling becomes 7'10'' when you measure. That means if you are using 5' turnings, the base must be 2'10'' in height. Another consideration you will have is whether or not you wish to attach the tops and bottoms of the posts to a shelflike board. I think using this type of board makes installation a lot simpler, besides adding a touch of decoration where the posts meet the ceiling.

Attach the turnings to the board by driving two nails from the underside of the board into the posts. You must use two nails in each post to keep it from turning and getting out of line as the result of use. It also helps to mark both boards before you start nailing the posts. Put the two

1 Room dividers can be easy to make. First, use either 2″ x 2″ or 2″ x 4″ lumber to build a frame. I used 2″ x 2″ uprights for this frame and made it 6″ wide by 4′ long.

2 Next, cover the frame with paneling. If the base is no more than 4′ wide, one sheet of paneling will cover it.

boards together; measure and mark on the edge of the board where each post must be fastened; then nail. By marking the two boards, you ensure that each post will be exactly vertical. I mounted the posts along the edge of both the bottom and top boards rather than centering them, so that the bottom board could be used as a shelf for books or as a place for potted plants. But once you have the posts nailed to the two boards, lift that section into place on top of the base cabinet and nail in place. As you can see in the illustration, using wood turnings for this sort of room divider does indeed make an unusual partition, and because of the turnings it does have a more professional look than an ordinary partition would have.

I'm sure there are hundreds of other ways that you could utilize similar materials in doing jobs around the house. Anytime you can come up with an idea that uses common materials, you'll save a lot of money and considerable work.

Natalie's Notes

In addition to looking for wood turnings at hardware stores and lumberyards, may I suggest scrounging around secondhand stores or even old houses that face a demolition crew. I've even seen some sold at auctions for a fraction of what you pay for new ones. Of course, you will probably have to paint them, since they are usually layered with several coats of varnish. This can cut down considerably on the cost of making a room divider—which frankly isn't something I would spend a great deal of money on. By the way, what ever happened to the old bead-curtain rage?

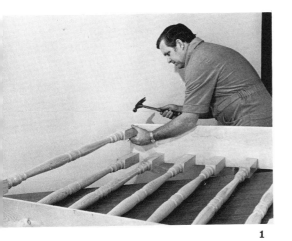

1

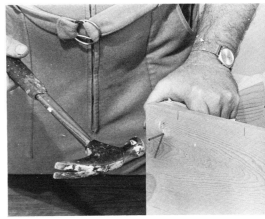

2

3

1 For the upper section of the room divider, I used wood turnings, which are available almost everywhere. Attach the uprights to boards, 8" wide and 1" thick, by nailing from the board into the turning. Put two nails into each turning to keep it from "turning."

2 This shows you where and how to drive the nails.

3 How about that! The top of the divider fits snug against the ceiling, and there is room on the shelf for books or potted plants. The turnings are expensive. This divider cost about $75.

7 SHELVING

There are so many different kinds of shelving that I hardly know where to begin. You can buy ready-made shelving of metal, wood, plastic and probably a dozen other kinds of materials and it will serve the purpose and give you added storage room or bookcases if you want to pay the price. Making your own shelving will save you a lot of money, but the most important reason for doing it yourself is that you can tailor the shelves to fit the space in your home instead of tailoring the space to fit the shelves.

If you have a limited number of tools available to do the job, it is always easier to draw up a rough idea of the dimensions of the finished product and have the lumberyard do the cutting to size for you. There may be a slight additional charge for this service, but it's worth it.

Let's imagine you're after more storage space in your apartment. I know what closets in apartments look like, because I've lived in one! But you can store more items in a closet on shelves than you can on hangers. Converting the closet to shelves is very easy, and you don't have to install any of the material permanently. Not only will you not damage any of the walls, but you can also take it with you if you decide to move.

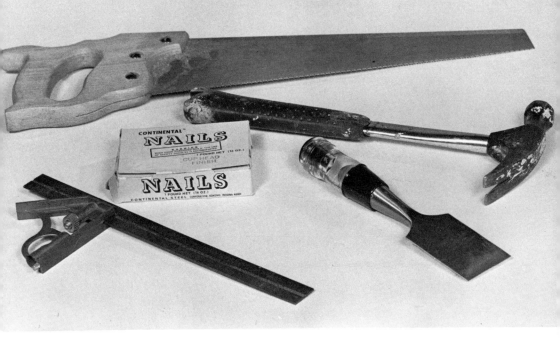

Basic tools for a shelf-making kit include a square, hammer, nails, chisel and handsaw. You might want to include a small block plane to remove the splinter hazard along the edges, and for longer-lasting results include some white glue.

Measure the inside of your closet for height, width and depth. Let's use hypothetical figures and say the closet is 4′ wide, 18″ deep and 5′ in height. Go to the lumberyard and buy one 4′ x 8′ sheet of ¾″ AD interior plywood. Have it cut into four strips 1′ wide by 4′ long. Cut the remainder of the plywood into 12″ squares (you'll get twelve of them). Get a box, or a pound, of 2″ finishing nails and a hammer, and you're in business!

The 1′ squares will be used as legs, one on either end of each 4′ length of plywood. Three or four nails driven from the top of the 4′ length of plywood into the 12″-square leg will be sufficient. Make four such sections and then stack them one on top of another in the closet. This will give you four shelves, 4′ long and 12″ deep. Simple? You bet! And you can figure out a similar plan for your own closet if you want to convert it to shelves. You can of course use only a couple of shelves at the bottom of the closet rather than filling the entire closet from top to bottom. But do it as you like and you'll discover that your closets get bigger with shelving. By the way, in case you're wondering what the other four pieces of 12"-square plywood are for that you have left over, use them as dividers down the middle of the shelving. They will strengthen the middle of the shelf board and won't even require nails. If you want to "pretty-up" the rough-sawed edges of the shelves, get some black plastic electrical tape and apply this over the edge. It will give the whole closet a more "finished" look, and it will keep splinters out of your fingers. For a fancier edge, various-colored tapes are available and in wide widths.

The most commonly needed shelving is additional bookcases, and people have been designing their own for years with all kinds of results. I guess bricks-and-boards is about the simplest kind you can build. You can vary the height of the shelves by adding more bricks, and you can make the unit as wide or as narrow as you want. The only problem with this sort of bookcase is that it takes a lot of bricks, and if you have to carry them very far they get awful heavy awful fast. But to make this type—just in case you've never seen one—stack the bricks on the floor at 3' intervals. You can make the shelves as far apart as you want by adding or subtracting a row of bricks. Place the board for your first shelf and then add bricks on top of the board till you reach the height you want for the next shelf, and so on. Four shelves high is usually just about the limit for this sort of construction. You can use a variety of materials other than bricks. I've seen the things constructed out of glass blocks, concrete blocks and even cut stone. I don't think they're particularly glamorous, but they are functional.

But regular bookcases aren't too tough to tackle if you

remember a few basics as you build them. It always simplifies construction if you utilize fairly standard sizes in your design. For example, a bookcase with dimensions of 4′ x 6′ will be easier to build and cost less than a bookcase 3′ x 5′10″. You might argue about the cost with me, but you can't argue about the work. One-by-eight-inch boards are ideal for bookcase building, and they are in plentiful supply. I would always recommend pine for this sort of thing, since all you're really going to see is the edge of the shelf. If you want something fancier than pine, you can cover it with wood-simulating tape or thin strips of wood veneer.

The secret of a sturdy bookcase is the back of the case— assuming, of course that you do not intend to nail the whole thing to the wall. One-quarter-inch plywood is perfect for bookcase backing, and since it is available in 4′ x 8′ sheets, you can adapt it to almost any usable dimension. Let's use the 4′ x 6′ bookcase as an example. The bookcase will be 4′ wide, and let's say you want the shelves to be about 10″ apart. Since the height of the bookcase will be 72″, such an arrangement will give you six shelves 10″ apart and one shelf 12″. Use the taller space in the 12″ shelf either at the bottom of the bookcase for larger books or at the top for art objects, etc.

Since you are using standard sizes, almost all of the lumber can be precut for you at the lumberyard. The ends of the bookcase are one-by-eights, 6′ long. One 12′ board cut in half gives you your ends. All of the shelves are 4′ long, and four 8′ boards cut in half will make all your shelves with one board to spare. Have the lumberyard cut the plywood 4′ x 6′ and you're in business.

The only other materials you'll need are ¾″ quarter-round molding, 1½″ finishing nails, white glue and a hammer. The quarter-round will adequately hold each shelf in place after it is nailed and glued to the ends of the bookcase. Make that your first step. Take the two boards that will be the ends of the bookcase and put them together on the floor edges up. Carefully mark on the edges with pencil where each shelf is to go. Turn the boards over and repeat the process on the opposite edges. (If you have a square, just do it once and then mark the ends accordingly.) If you don't want to do any cutting at all, you can have the lumberyard cut the quarter-round molding into 7″ lengths. (They may laugh, but they'll do it!) Now decide which is the top and which is the bottom of the two ends. Put the boards flat on the floor, side by side. Quarter-round molding is flat on two sides and round on the other. Put one flat side against the bookcase end board, so that the other flat side makes a minishelf which will hold the shelf board. Line up the quarter-round with the edge markings, apply the white glue to the edge of the quarter-round that will be against the end of the bookcase and put it in place. Now drive three nails through the quarter-round into the bookcase end. Repeat the process on all strips of quarter-round.

Now you should have the quarter-round strips on both end pieces of the bookcase. Step 2 is the installation of the top of the bookcase. Take that extra shelf board and use it as the very top shelf on the bookcase. No quarter-round is needed for this one, but you can use it if you like. Put the two end boards on edge, put the top-shelf board on edge and insert it **between** the two end pieces. Nail it in place. Now, take the piece of plywood, already cut to 4′ x 6′, slip it over the three pieces of wood and align the three pieces so they fit the plywood exactly. Nail the backing to the three pieces of wood. Now stand the bookcase up, insert the other shelves and you've completed the hard part!

You can finish the bookcase by painting, staining or

1 Shelving can be as simple or as complicated as you want to make it. For example, a simple shelf, ideal for basement storage. First, hold the two boards together that will be the two ends of the shelving. Use a square to draw a line across both boards where you want the shelf. Turn the boards over to the other edge and repeat the procedure. This way the shelf boards will be level and square.

2 Use the marks on the boards as a guide and run a bead of glue where the shelf brackets will be nailed into the end uprights.

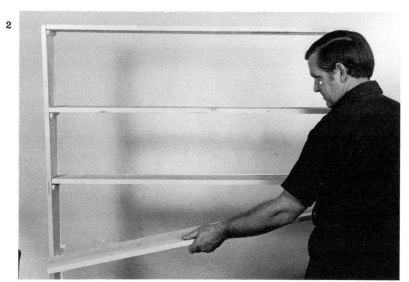

1 I used 1″ quarter-round as the shelf brackets. Press the quarter-round down into the glue and then nail into place. (Glue makes a much stronger bond than just nailing. The only real purpose of the nails is to hold the two pieces of wood tightly together until the glue dries.)

2 Glue and nail all pieces of quarter-round in place and then you're ready for assembly. I start at the top and again use glue to attach the boards. Nail directly into the ends of the shelf boards. For a free-standing shelf arrangement you will need a plywood or hardboard backing. It can be nailed onto the completed shelving and will add considerable strength. (Make the bookcase a maximum of 4′ in overall width so that a standard sheet of plywood will fit without extensive cutting.)

shellacking. No matter what you do to the shelves and end pieces, I would suggest that you paint the backboard of the bookcase a flat black. Inexpensive fir plywood looks better black in my opinion, and in bookcases, a black background is more attractive to me. But see, it isn't that tough to do, and again may I suggest making your own variations now that you know something about the very basics of bookcase construction.

Natalie's Notes

It's really amazing what the friendly neighborhood lumberyard will do for a helpless female.

And once all the measuring and cutting is done, putting together a bookcase such as the one Wally describes is both simple and fun.

I'm not particularly fond of stained pine, so I would suggest painting the wood. I've seen some pretty wild bookcases done in all sorts of bright colors, and if you have the right apartment or house, it's quite effective.

The shelves Wally suggests are a boon to anyone who's ever lived in an apartment. And even if you move and have no use for them anymore, your investment was certainly worthwhile.

8 FLOORS—STRIPPING AND SANDING

Pine Floors

Next to painting, working on floors—whether you're stripping, sanding or refinishing—has to be the most frustrating and difficult job of all. Obviously, I hate it! I would rather climb around on a slate roof than strip an old wide-plank floor, and since I have done both, I do indeed know what I'm talking about. Maybe the reason I feel so strongly on this subject is that I once started stripping 5,000 square feet of wide-plank pine floors with steel wool and ammonia. For weeks I worked on my hands and knees, with my wonderful, blue-blooded wife right beside me. I gagged on ammonia fumes, ran long splinters into my hands and cursed the day we ever bought the house. After we finished the first floor, comprising 2,500 square feet, I resolved to carpet the upstairs rather than go through a divorce. My knees were horribly swollen, and I'll wager that today that house still has an ammonia smell to it!

But if you face a similar situation, I know that you won't

be able to resist the temptation to strip those wide-plank pine floors and restore them to their original beauty.

A few words of advice at the beginning. If you really want to preserve the character of an antique house and the full beauty of old floors, you can't sand floors and have them look anything but new. The age marks, the black spots, the heel indentations really add to the beauty of wide-plank pine! By stripping such a floor, you can retain most of those marks; if you sand it, you lose them. It is also difficult to sand most old wide-plank floors, because some, if not all, of the boards will be cupped and bowed, and the sanding belt will tend to gouge into the imperfections. Most old floors were also surface-nailed instead of blind-nailed, which means that wrought-iron, square-headed nails were driven into the face of the floorboards and are visible to the eye. These nails play havoc with sanding belts. (Blind nailing is driving the nails into the edges of each board when they are installed, so that they are not seen on the surface of the floor.)

I would not recommend tackling 2,500 square feet of flooring all at one time, but room by room might not be so bad. We tried everything on our floors. At first we used a commercial paint remover and spent a fortune. The product we used did indeed do the job, but it cost about $5 a gallon. On the basis of ten gallons per room, that gets expensive fast! We then tried TSP, a dry chemical powder sold by good paint stores. TSP stands for trisodium phosphate, which is the main ingredient in most commercial paint removers and is even used in most household cleansers.

Add about one cup of TSP to two gallons of boiling water and you have a potent remover. Mop the TSP onto the floor, let it stand fifteen or twenty minutes, then mop up the old finish with rags, mops or what-have-you. But even

TSP left something to be desired on our floors, which had been given a black-looking finish 125 years ago. The old finish was probably a shellac base with pigment added. The floors had also been stained under the shellac. Anyway, the TSP did very well in some areas, and didn't work at all on other parts.

Finally, we resorted to household ammonia and steel wool. The fumes are horrible—so horrible that we mounted an electric fan on the floor to keep them away from us as we worked. Make sure you buy the regular ammonia, not the sudsy kind, and use it straight as it comes from the bottle. Pour about a cupful on the floor, lean back and take a deep breath and, with your hands in rubber gloves, grasp a chunk of steel wool and start rubbing the ammonia on the finish. The ammonia will not evaporate quickly, so you can rub until you see the old finish dissolving. Then take an old rag and wipe off the residue of finish. You might have to go over the same area a couple of times, but it will work. After you have gone over the entire room, let the floor dry thoroughly, at least a couple of days.

If the floor was stained prior to finishing (shellacking or varnishing), you will still have to get rid of the old stain before the floor is going to look like pine. I recommend bleaching the old stain out of the wood by using another rather common household product. Most brands of liquid bleach, such as Clorox or Purex, work beautifully. They will not bleach the wood lighter than it was originally, and they work fast. First, make sure the floor has dried **thoroughly**—twenty-four hours or longer—from the application of ammonia. (This is **important**!) Then pour some bleach into an old bucket and, using a mop you can spare, apply the bleach to the floor full strength. Give the entire floor a generous soaking. Then put the mop back into the bucket before it dissolves, and wait about five minutes.

1   2

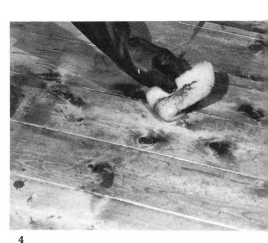

3   4

1 Stripping floors with ammonia is mostly hard work! Use regular household ammonia, rubber gloves, steel wool and old rags to wipe up the mess.

2 Pour the ammonia directly onto the surface to be stripped. Let the chemical stand on the old finish for a minute or so before you try to remove it.

3 Use the steel-wool pad to remove the old finish by rubbing with the grain. The fumes are terrible! You must have plenty of ventilation in the room. Rub until you can see that the old finish has dissolved.

4 Wipe the residue from the floor. Sometimes it will take more than one application of ammonia to remove thickly encrusted old finishes. If the floor still appears too dark after you have removed the surface finish, **let the wood dry thoroughly,** then use regular household bleach, full strength, to restore the wood to its natural color.

Really, the bleach will do about all it's going to do in a couple of minutes. Now, take clear water and flush the floor, then mop it up as best you can. Let the floor dry for another couple of days and you'll have an almost-white pine floor, complete with age marks. The surface of the floor may be just a little fuzzy from the harsh chemicals, so you really should go over it again with steel wool to remove the wood fibers that are now standing on their heads. After you have removed the "fuzz," vacuum the floor and you're ready for what seems like Step 1,001.

First, you must decide whether you want the floor natural or wish to stain it before you add the final finish. To see how the floor will look with just a clear finish, wet a section with water and you will get an exact idea of what the floor will look like without stain. (It will be very light!) We did not want light floors in our house, so we stained them with our witches' brew of a red-cherry hue.

If you decide to stain, it's going to be trial and error. Paint stores handle every conceivable kind of stain in almost every color of the rainbow. Your personal preference should be your only consideration in selecting a color for your floor. We used a McCloskey oil stain called Antique Cherry, but added a red pigment called "H" in the quantity of "8." This did not really give us red floors, but it did give a slight red cast to the brown cherry stain which we thought was attractive.

The length of time you leave the stain on the floor will determine the penetration of the stain and the richness of the color. I like to stain floors using rubber gloves and a rag. Pour the stain into a plastic bucket, dip the rag into the stain—get it real juicy—and spread the stain on the floor in big, sweeping moves. In our case, I let the stain stand for about five minutes before I took clean rags and wiped the residue from the floor. (You stain and let your wife wipe about five minutes behind you.) You have to wipe it before it dries; otherwise you'll end up with a gooey mess. After you have stained and wiped the entire floor, let it dry quietly! Don't walk on it! Forget the room is in the house for at least two days! Keep the dogs away from it, lock your kids in their rooms—in other words, do whatever is necessary to keep the room vacated.

After the floor has dried, you will probably notice a couple of areas where it was not wiped well enough and it looks smudged. Steel-wool those places very carefully to remove the excess stain. (If the color is horrible, your wife is threatening a divorce and your kids are crying, throw another bottle of bleach on the floor and you're back where you started.) The people who make stains claim you can quit at this point if you want to. I don't believe them! I think you should take one more step before you hang up your rubber gloves, and your wife will love you for it. Give the entire floor a couple of coats of polyurethane finish. Don't argue with me, just do it! Vacuum the stained floor first. Get an old lamp and put it on the floor so that the light is facing you. (This way you can see what you're doing as you apply the polyurethane to the floor.) You can brush on this clear-plastic-varnish–like stuff, or you can apply it with a wax applicator. It won't get bubbles, and it flows beautifully! Apply the first coat and let it dry for about twenty hours. Buff it lightly with fine-grade steel wool and then apply the second coat. Magnificent! You can take your choice as to the degree of gloss you want on the floor; polyurethane comes in dull, satin or high-gloss finish. We used satin and loved it. If you use a high gloss and find it too shiny, you can always go over it with steel wool and arrive at the degree of gloss you prefer.

Hardwood Floors

Now we're in a different ball game! Hardwood floors lend themselves to sanding for a number of reasons. First, they are usually narrow boards nailed tightly together. The wood itself is hard enough so that age marks are of no consequence, and therefore you will not lose any "character" of the floor by sanding. If the floor has been loused up with a thick gooey finish, strip it chemically before sanding, as a thick finish will quickly gum up a sandpaper belt. You can use TSP, ammonia, a commercial paint remover or whatever you like best. If the floor has had only two or three coats of a clear finish, then go ahead and sand.

Sanding machines are available at most rental stores, and this is by far the best move to make. You can rent the big belt sanding machine and the edger for $4 or $5 a day. You'll have to pay extra for the sanding belts and disks you use. I usually get three grades of belts for the floor machine—starting the job with a coarse paper, then going to a medium and finishing the job with a fine grade. With disks for the edge sander you should follow the same procedure. You have to learn how to handle a floor-sanding machine simply by doing it, and the best advice I can give you is to take your time until you get the feel of it. The first floor I sanded looked as wavy as the Atlantic Ocean when I finished because I hadn't had sense enough to always keep the machine in motion when I had the sanding belt turning. Always keep the machine in motion; sand parallel to the boards in the floor, never across them, and if you want to stop and rest, turn off the machine and wait until the belt stops turning before you let it rest against the floor.

Sanding a floor accomplishes at least two things. Not

1

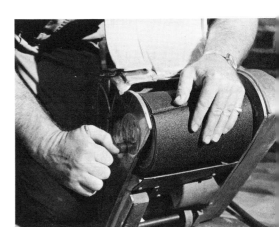

4

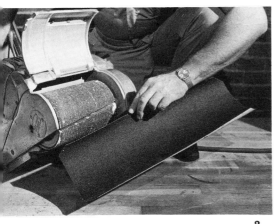

2

5

3

1 This is the type of floor-sanding machine you can rent from many of the franchised rental stores. Notice that I have both hands on the handles.

2 The floor-sanding machine is really just a "drum sander." Sanding belts are placed on the drum, which revolves at high speed. The weight of the machine is sufficient to hold the drum against the surface of the floor.

3 You will have to change belts several times before the job is complete. A wrench is supplied with the machine which opens the sanding drum sort of like a clamshell.

4 Remove the old belt. Now feed the new belt around the drum and place one end of the sandpaper belt into the slot. Hold that end in place and insert the other end also.

5 Now tighten the wrench, which in turn closes the "clamshell" drum and draws the sanding belt tight.

only does it remove old finishes, but it also levels the irregularities that make the floor uneven. You shouldn't encounter protruding nails in a hardwood floor, but in case you do, countersink the nails below the surface of the floor using a hammer and a nail punch. This way the protruding nails will not snag the sandpaper belt.

You'll discover that the big floor-sanding machine will not sand all the way to the wall. You'll be lucky to get within 3″ of the baseboard with the big machine, and that's why you have the circular edge sander. The edge sander is a real tiger! It has a double hand grip, and you'll need both hands to hold on to the thing once you've turned it on. Approach this job with caution until you get the hang of it. The sandpaper disk will really cut into the floor if you try to apply too much pressure. Start out nice and gentle, then increase pressure on the disk as your confidence increases. Again, I start with a coarse grade of paper, then a medium grade, followed by a fine grade. The harder you sand with the coarse grade, the more marks you will leave in the floor and the harder they will be to remove. Another tough aspect of using an edge sander is that you're sanding cross-grain and the circular action of the sandpaper will tend to leave ring marks on the floor. You may have to go around the edges by hand with sand paper to remove them. Just take your time and don't let the edge sander get away from you.

There are a number of rather disgusting side effects every time you sand a floor. I don't care what anyone else tells you, the house is going to be a mess! Both sanding machines usually have dust bags similar to those of a vacuum cleaner, but they don't get all of the dust. Be sure to check the bags frequently and empty them whenever they are half full. Forewarn your wife that a fine layer of dust will cover everything in the house.

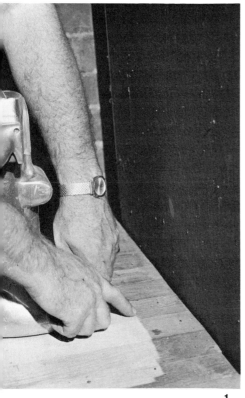 

1   2

1 The big floor-sanding machine will not sand around the edges of the room. You'll find that 2″–3″ of unsanded floor must be done with an edge-sanding machine. The two units are usually rented as a pair.

2 The edge sander is designed to fit tightly against the wall or baseboard. Grasp the two handles firmly, and use only light downward pressure. The edge sander is a circular sander, which means you are sanding against the grain of the wood. Do it carefully and the circular sanding marks will be less noticeable.

1

2

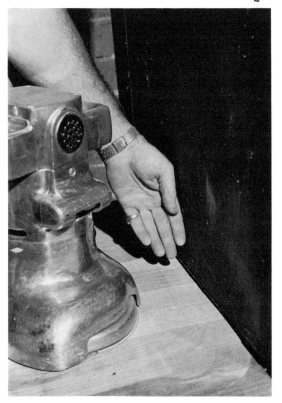

1 You'll have to change the sandpaper several times on the edge sander also. A wrench is supplied with the sander. Use the wrench to loosen the bolt. Remove both the bolt and the washer. Place the new sanding disk on the sander, insert the bolt and washer into the hole in the disk and thread the bolt into the base of the machine.

2 This shows how well the edge sander does its job. The only place it cannot be used is in corners. Each corner of the room will have to be hand-sanded.

Finishing hardwood floors is not any different from finishing any other kind. You will discover that hardwood will not take a stain as readily as pine floors, because the pores of hardwood are smaller and the stain will not penetrate as easily. Since hardwood flooring is usually oak, let's presume that's what you're faced with. For a natural finish, your paint store will have a variety of products all of which are relatively easy to apply. Most finishes can be either brushed on or applied with a lamb's-wool applicator. Either way works quite well as long as you don't leave puddles of the finish on the floor. It is very important to have a good light source when you apply the finish. I still prefer a polyurethane for floors, but ask your paint dealer to show you what other kinds of finishes are available. Sometimes it is easier to use a colored finish coat than to try to stain a hardwood floor, particularly if you are after a dark color. Dark floors are attractive, but they do show footprints much easier than a lighter color.

Some amateurs like to oil a floor with something like linseed oil. I wouldn't recommend it. The floor will eventually turn almost black. Dust and dirt will stick to it like glue, and it will get very dull. Remember the old grocery stores that had oiled floors? Ugh. Also, an oiled floor can be a fire hazard. It's your floor, though, and you can do anything you want to do provided your spouse agrees!

Natalie's Notes

All ye seekers of the truth will be interested to know that Wally's "wonderful, blue-blooded wife" was not only right beside him: she actually did most of the messy work. He discovered early on that ammonia had a less drastic effect on me, and I must admit I soon became a first-class "stripper."

Yes, the floors did turn out beautifully, with all those lovely age marks that W.B. finds attractive in floors but not in wives. Unless you live in a mansion, it is almost imperative that you take a room at a time, since that room is absolutely out of bounds for at least four days. It is also advisable to keep close tabs on children and animals—or better yet, send them to Grandma's and the kennel (respectively, of course) till the job is done.

Although I try to blot out the memory, I recall that we decided to tackle the job in early August, and the week we picked set new records for highs in temperature. I would not recommend undertaking the job in summer. As a matter of fact, I would not recommend undertaking the job at all—unless you are like us, crazy about beautiful old floors.

9 VINYL, ASBESTOS AND RUBBER FLOOR TILES

Installing New Tile

I used to look at the advertisements in magazines that picture sensational-looking tile floors done in wild geometric designs with fancy borders, with a caption reading, "You too can do your own floor." Ha! Those floors were installed by guys who do nothing else and who followed a design laid out by an architect, backed up by an engineer and a mathematician.

But an average floor you can do! You can put in a vinyl-tile floor, for example, and save yourself a good sum of money. Sure, you can include a reasonable amount of "customizing" if you choose, but don't ever expect to see the floor pictured in **Better Homes and Gardens.** Installing a tile floor is a messy job. You won't get it done in an average weekend, and the preparation will take longer than actually installing the new floor.

How you begin to install tile depends on what kind of floor you have. If the floor already has tile on it, the old tile should be covered or come off. If the floor has inlaid linoleum or some other kind of composition covering, this too should be covered or removed. But if the floor is wooden boards, you have yet another problem.

Let's assume you have wooden boards, and we'll talk of the other types of flooring as we go. A good rule to follow with a board floor (even hardwood) is never to place tile directly over the boards. No matter how tight the old floor appears, no matter how small the cracks may be between the boards and no matter how well you countersink the old nails, it's all going to show right through the new tile in a matter of weeks! To do a good job, it is almost imperative to use some sort of underlayment board over the old floor. Underlayment board can be almost any good ¼″ material, such as hardboard or plywood. Since both are sold in standard 4′ x 8′ sheets, have the material cut to 4′ squares before you bring it home. Or your lumberyard may sell ⅛″ hardboard underlayment already cut to 4′ squares.

Stagger the seams as much as possible, and buy special underlayment-board nails to attach the material to the floor. Tile manufacturers recommend that you nail into the board at 6″ intervals at most, to make sure that you eliminate as much "give" as possible. I mean every 6″ all over the board, not just around the edges. You must cover every square foot of the floor and piece the underlayment board in places like under radiators, etc. Since the underlayment board is ⅛″ or ¼″ thick, and the tile may be as thick as ⅛″ or 3/16″, you may have raised the surface of your floor as much as ½″ after you're finished. You must trim the bottom of doors if they drag over the new surface.

If the old floor was linoleum or tile, you have a couple of options. First, you can remove the old covering, scrape off the old adhesive that held it in place and then, if underlayment board was used originally, you can put the new floor down over it. My advice would be to go with option No. 2, which is to leave the old floor as it is and install new underlayment board right over the top of the old floor covering. One of the essential requisites for a smooth finished job is having a smooth surface to install the new tiles on. If you remove the old floor covering, you must get every bit of tile, adhesive, dirt, grime and grit removed before you place new tiles on the floor. It's very hard to get all the grit off, and as I mentioned, every little lump is going to show sooner or later.

When the underlayment board is down, you're ready to begin with the new tiles. Everyone says you must always start in the center of the room when you're installing this sort of floor covering. Let me give you a couple of exceptions to that rule. If you are using a one-color pattern as opposed to a checkerboard design, you can start almost anywhere and the physical appearance of the room will not be affected. If you really don't care about having the center of the design in the exact center of the room, also forget it. But if you're trying to save some money by making the tile go as far as it will go, then again you will want to start in the center. The reason is apparent once someone explains it to you. So, here I go!

If you start in the center of the room, and lay your tiles side by side until you reach both walls, the tile that adjoins the wall will probably be a part tile. In other words, a full tile will not fit without being cut. What you are striving for is equal-width tiles in the perimeter row. A room does look a little strange if the last row of tiles along the north side of a room is 4″ wide, the west side 8″ wide, the south side 6″ wide and the east side 1″ wide! It's a much nicer-looking job if all of the perimeter tiles are 4″ wide. Besides, you don't waste as much material, because what is left over from one side will fit on the other side of a room.

Another reason for starting in the center of the room is to have perfectly straight rows of tile. The easiest tool for finding the center is a chalk line, but any piece of string will do. Take the string or chalk line and extend it catercorner across the room. Take another piece of string and run it catercorner the other way. The string is now across the floor in a large X. The point where the strings intersect is the exact center, and this is where the first tile should be placed. Put a mark on the center of the floor. Then draw a straight line across the middle of the room. You'll line up your tiles along this. Now you're ready to apply the adhesive.

This has to be the gooiest, stickiest stuff ever imagined! Wear old clothes, have a lot of old rags and try to keep your hands and fingers clean so you don't smear the stuff on the face of the tiles. Tile dealers will recommend a trowel to apply the mastic; buy the cheapest one they offer, because it will be thrown away after the job. The tile trowel has sawtooth notches along one edge which will distribute just enough adhesive to the floor to adequately hold the tile without squishing up through the cracks. I usually apply the adhesive to about four or five square feet of the floor before installing the tiles. It takes several hours for the adhesive to harden, so it's difficult to get too far ahead of yourself. Don't put the adhesive on the floor over a greater area than an arm's length, because you will have to reach that far to put each tile in place.

Take the first tile and carefully press it in place over the mark at the center of the floor. Even if your pattern is all one color, there will still be a sort of grain in the tile, and this grain should be alternated with each piece. Press the tiles firmly in place, and wipe any excess adhesive off the face of the tiles and around the cracks before the adhesive

1 Apply the floor-tile mastic with a notched trowel so that you get a uniform coating. The area where the mastic is applied must be thoroughly cleaned and leveled before the tile is installed.

2 After the mastic is spread, set each tile in place; then press firmly on the tile so that it will settle onto the mastic. Avoid getting mastic on the surface of the tile.

3 Anyone can do a professional-type job when it comes to fitting and cutting tiles. To determine the exact size needed to fill this space, first place the tile directly over the tile already on the floor.

1 Place a third tile on top of the other two. Allow the top tile to fit against the baseboard, or in this case the built-in cabinet. Now take a pencil and trace along the edge of the top tile, which in turn marks the second tile for cutting. Doing it this way ensures a perfect fit.

2 Natalie happened to pick a product called Fritztile for one of our bathrooms, and you can't cut it as easily as the regular types of tile. This product has real marble chips embedded in a vinyl substance. I used an electric jigsaw and many blades before the job was complete.

dries. Continue applying mastic and tiles until all that is left to do is the outside perimeter of the room.

A pure-vinyl tile is the easiest of all to cut, and you can use a sharp knife or a heavy-duty pair of scissors. I find a razor-blade knife preferable for this kind of work. If the tile is rubber, the razor knife will also work, though the job is a little harder. If you're using asphalt tile you'll have to first heat the tile with a propane-type torch until it softens; then it too can be cut with a knife.

A couple of other tips about laying tile: Make a couple of kneepads out of some old rags before you start. It's also nice to have a straightedge to use when you cut the tile— ideally, a framing square. And after you're all finished with your installation, it will also help to use a roller rented from a tile store to make sure all edges of each tile are firmly in contact with the adhesive. The floor roller is a miniversion of a lawn roller, usually heavy iron, and does a better job than you can do by hand. Tiling is a messy undertaking, but you can do it if you try!

Replacing Tile

One of the easiest repairs to make in a home is the replacement of worn or broken floor tiles, and the procedure is much the same regardless of what the tile material is. The secret of doing a nice job is to have a few pieces of tile left over from the original installation. You may think you're buying a very standard pattern when you get the tile, only to be disappointed a couple of years later when you learn it has been discontinued. If you're lucky you may be able to make a match, but even then the replacement tile will be from a different "lot" and chances are there will be a slight color variation. But even a tile that

1

3

2

1 Good shears will also cut most tiles if you need an irregular shape.

2 More commonly used tiles are made of vinyl, and they are easily cut with a "utility knife."

3 Notice that I use a steel yardstick as a straightedge. However, always put the edge you cut next to the wall, using the factory edge of the tile to butt against another tile. No matter how straight a line you think you have cut, it will not be perfect.

does not match perfectly is better than one that has a corner cracked off, or one that has badly discolored. The procedure I use is similar to that for replacement of ceramic tiles. The tools required include a propane torch, a stiff putty knife, a replacement tile and a small amount of tile adhesive.

With the propane torch, carefully heat the tile that you wish to remove. Hold the tip of the torch about 4″ from the surface of the tile, because the tile material will burn if you apply too much heat in any one place. The adhesive that holds the tile to the floor is also flammable, so don't try to burn the tile or you might lose the whole house. Also, be careful not to let the flame come in contact with any of the adjoining tiles, because they will discolor.

After about two minutes of applied heat, the tile is ready to remove. Take a stiff putty knife and start in the center of the tile you wish to remove, so as not to disturb the edges of the surrounding tiles; gouge the tile with an edge of the knife and work the knife underneath it. Or if the tile has been completely loosened by the heat, you can pry it upward from an edge. If you meet considerable resistance in prying the tile loose from the floor, then you need still more heat. The tile will get very soft with the right application of heat and is easily removed.

After you have taken the tile up from the floor, scrape the floor surface with the knife and remove as much of the old adhesive as you can. Make sure you remove any foreign particles that may have fallen into the area where you removed the tile, because even little pieces of hardened adhesive will eventually show through the face of the replacement tile. Now, take the replacement tile and, after applying a thin coat of new adhesive to the floor, press it into place. Carefully remove any adhesive that has

The only tools you'll need to replace a floor tile are a stiff chisel, a propane torch, mastic and the replacement tile.

This chipped floor tile can easily be replaced provided you have an extra tile.

A butane torch gets the job done faster because of its intense heat. Play the flame from the torch directly on the defective tile until the tile starts to curl. Be careful not to let the flame come in contact with adjoining tiles, because the heat will loosen and discolor them.

Slide a wide-blade putty knife under the tile and gently pry it loose from the floor. The heat from the torch will have softened the mastic that holds the tile to the floor.

Off it comes! Usually in one piece.

Scrape away the old mastic with a putty knife, and be sure to remove all dirt particles that may have dropped into the area. Get it nice and clean!

Use the putty knife to spread new mastic on the floor. A thin coating will do the job, about 1/16″ thick.

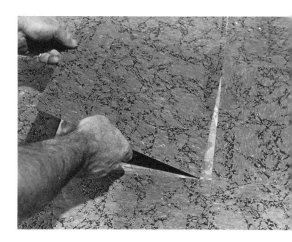

Carefully insert the replacement tile into the space and press firmly in place.

Even though you firmly pressed the new tile when you installed it, it's also a good idea to weight it down with several books or anything flat and heavy.

squished up to the surface through the cracks and your tile has been replaced.

Natalie's Notes

I agree with Wally that putting down floor tiles wouldn't get my vote for "fun" job of the year. But think of all the money you save—which, to be truthful, was what kept us down on our hands and knees. I must admit, I managed to make myself scarce the day or two Wally tackled the underlayment-board installation, but I got in on the gooey business of laying tiles. There is only one word of advice I can add: persevere! You'll be glad you did.

10 SLATE FLOORS

One of my troubles is the fact that I come from a long line of muleheaded people. My ancestors were of German extraction, and probably a couple of them were Dutch. And Natalie is convinced that there must be a couple of Scotsmen in the background, because I do occasionally pinch a penny. But that combination was what led me to installing a slate floor in the side entrance hall of that old mansion in upstate New York. I was fortunate in having a very heavy and solid floor to work with, even though you could look through cracks into the cellar. Anytime you start installing a rigid floor like slate, you must know that the subfloor can support it without flexing and allowing the grout or mortar joints to break out. Unless the house is falling apart, and I mean really falling apart, you should be able to use slate without monumental problems.

Natalie wanted slate. She wouldn't settle for the vinyl stuff that looks like slate; she wanted the real thing. I don't know where you live, but in New York, guys who install slate floors spend every winter in Florida! The easiest kind to install is called Vermont slate, random size, random color, with red. This has been milled at the stone

This is my slate-floor-installation kit. You'll need underlayment board, rubber gloves, a notched trowel, mastic, grout, sponge, squeegee, hacksaw with abrasive blade, glass cutter, straightedge, paintbrush, electric circular saw with stone-cutting blade, a couple of buckets and several rags.

quarry to either ¼″ or ⅜″ thickness. The reason this is necessary is so that the slate can be applied with a mastic instead of in a mortar bed. When you use varying thicknesses of stone or slate, you must have sufficient depth in mortar for the surface to end up flat and level. With milled slate, you know that if you install the slate on a flat surface, the top side will also be flat. For interior flooring, always use milled slate.

The biggest expense in the slate is freight. If you live in the northeastern part of the United States it is quite inexpensive. It will cost twice as much in the Midwest, and you'll have to hold your breath on the West Coast. It generally comes packaged by the box, ten square feet per package. The pattern is printed on the carton, and putting it together is like working an easy jigsaw puzzle. I would recommend installing underlayment board before you begin. This should be ¼″ in thickness and can be either exterior plywood or hardboard. I used the regular ¼″ exterior plywood and found it to be satisfactory. Anyway, decide on what you want to use and cover the area that you wish to slate with the board. Get the kind of nails that won't pop out after a couple of weeks. In fact, they're called underlayment nails. Nail about 8″ apart everywhere on the board. I find it easier to buy the board in 4′ x 8′ sheets, then saw each one in half and put them down in 4′ sections. Stagger the seams on the 4′ sections and nail them down tight enough so that you cannot see the board "give" when you walk across it.

Use the same type of mastic for slate that you would use for ceramic tile. The tile store where you get your slate will recommend a brand. Use a notched trowel with ⅛″ teeth. **No bigger!** The salesman will try to tell you that you need a heavier coat of mastic on the floor. He's wrong! Spread the mastic on an area that still enables you to reach the farthest point. Don't worry about the mastic drying faster than you can lay the slate; it takes six to eight hours for most mastics to set up firmly. Make sure that every bit of floor is covered with the rippled effect that your notched trowel will give.

If you want a professional-looking floor, you should start in the center of the room. Establish that point by running two pieces of string corner to corner, corner to corner in the shape of an X. Where the strings cross is the center point, and this is where the center of the slate pattern should be. The reason to start in the center is so that the pieces which go against the wall will be of equal width on both sides of the room. If you don't do this, you might have a 2″ strip of slate along one wall and a 5″ strip along the other. That never particularly bothered me, but if you want the floor perfectly centered, you have to start in the center.

When you have the mastic down, start putting the pieces of slate in place. Keep the pattern from the box before you at all times. After ten or fifteen minutes it may become more and more difficult to distinguish one size of slate from another. There isn't any real tragedy if you deviate from the pattern, but it can complicate the job. The hardest part is maintaining a grout joint that is even between all of the tiles. Some recommend ⅜", others ½", and I say ⅝" between all tiles. It's a question of taste. I gauge this with my eye, checking it once in a while with a rule as I move along, but I don't find it necessary to measure each crack. As you put each piece of slate into place, press down firmly so that the piece is flat and so that it has good contact with the mastic.

The easiest way to cut the slate, I found, was to use my electric handsaw. Anything that has a 6" or larger circular blade will do the job. Buy a special stone-cutting blade from your hardware store for about $3; then you can cut slate the same way you cut wood. You get a lot of stone dust as you saw through each piece, so be sure you've locked the lady of the house in another room before you start to saw.

NEVER go near a stone-cutting job without safety glasses.

If you don't have an electric saw, you can use a hacksaw with a carborundum round blade, but it becomes tiresome pretty fast. Convince your wife that all of the money you're saving on labor offsets the purchase of a saw.

Try not to get mastic on the face of the slate from sticky fingers and accidental droppings. Most tile stores sell mastic solvent, and it's a heck of a lot easier to clean that stuff off before it cures.

O.K., you have all of the slate in place and your wife is telling you what a great job you've done and is already

1

2

3

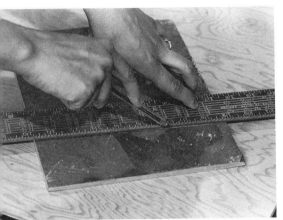

4   5

1 The underlayment board is the first step in installing slate over an existing floor. Step 2 is shown here. Apply the gooey mastic with a notched trowel. I prefer the notches to be ⅛″ deep, to leave a rather heavy coating of mastic on the floor. Cover an area of about four or five square feet, apply the slate, then coat another area, etc.

2 A suggested pattern is included on the slate carton, and you're ahead of the game if you stick to that pattern. Make sure the flat side of the slate is the one that is placed against the mastic. First put it in its approximate position in the mastic.

3 At this point the mastic is still soft enough to let you slide the piece of slate until you have it aligned with the other pieces. Leave a grout crack between pieces not less than ⅜″ wide or more than ⅝″. The width of the grout crack is personal preference within the tolerances given. If you decide on a ½″ crack, keep it ½″ throughout the entire floor.

4 No matter how much planning goes into the installation, you'll still have to cut some pieces. First measure the size piece needed and mark the slate by scratching a line where the cut must be made. A nail works well as a mark scratcher.

5 Try to do this outdoors if possible. The special fiber blade in the saw makes short work of cutting slate, but the cloud of dust generated will not be appreciated by the lady of the house. For smaller cutting jobs, such as notching a small hole to fit around a pipe, use the hacksaw with a round abrasive blade.

talking about a slate floor in the bathroom. Forget the floor for twenty-four hours. Soak your knees in hot water and have your wife rub your back. **Don't walk on the floor.** Keep the dogs and kids off the floor too.

After twenty-four hours, check five or six pieces by trying gently to move them. If the mastic has set up properly, you won't be able to even jiggle them. The next step is applying sealer. There are a variety of kinds of sealers available for stone. Brush it on with a wax applicator, or with a rag wrapped around a broom. It's a thin, watery stuff, and you can do an entire floor in just a few minutes. Let it dry thoroughly and put on another coat. And then another.

Now you're ready to grout. The first time I did this, some idiot sold me vinyl grout, which I used according to instructions and which I shall never forget. The grout mixed beautifully and went on smoothly, and two weeks later Natalie and I were still on our hands and knees, garbed in rubber boots and rubber gloves, using steel wool and muriatic acid trying to get the grout off the surface of the slate. Maybe there is some way to use this stuff, but I failed to discover it. Use regular mortar grout and save yourself a lot of grief. As the years go by, the mortar grout will flake and chip out of the joints and you'll have to replace some of it, but that isn't as bad as what we had to do.

Mix the dry grout powder with water until you have a thick, gooey mess. The consistency should be thicker than whipped cream but thinner than mashed potatoes. Use a 6″ or 8″ rubber squeegee to spread the grout over the tile and force it into the cracks. Don't get in a hurry; the grout won't set up completely for several hours. Don't get any more grout on the face of the slate than is absolutely necessary. Wipe off the excess from the face before you move to another area. When you do this, you'll find that you are

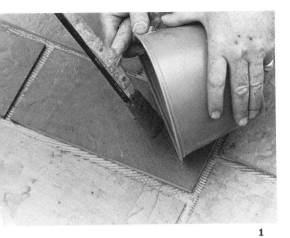

1

2

3

1 Before you start to grout slate, be certain that the mastic has dried and the slate is firmly adhered to the floor. Also, since slate is not a glazed tile, it is important that the slate be coated before grouting. You can use either a liquid stone sealer or polyurethane-type varnish. I prefer the latter. Either way, give the slate at least two coats before attempting to grout, and be certain that the sealer or polyurethane is **completely dry.** You can really have a mess if the polyurethane has not dried completely. Are you ready? Mix the grout powder with water according to package directions and begin!

2 Draw the squeegee diagonally over the cracks to completely fill them with grout.

3 Use a wide, flat sponge slightly dampened with water to remove the excess grout from the face of the slate. This is the hardest part of all. As you wipe with the sponge, you'll tend to wipe the grout joint as well, which in turn spreads even more grout on the face. Do it carefully, and with patience plus a lot of wiping you'll succeed. (What is left on the face of the slate usually dries white or gray, and, yes, it must all come off! Sorry about that.)

disturbing the grout in the cracks as well. Use your finger to smooth out the ruffles in the cracks, and let the grout set semihard before you try to remove the remainder from the face. Since the grout is either gray or white in color, I can assure you that any grout left on the face of the slate will show when it dries. Some you won't be able to get off, but most of it will come off with steel wool. After you've grouted all of the cracks, worry about what you didn't get off the face of the slate. At this point, that's all you can do!

When the grout has set up and hardened in the cracks, then begin in earnest to clean the surface. If you have a lot on the surface, you'll have to use muriatic acid to thoroughly clean it off. That is hot stuff, so be **very, very careful.** You must use rubber gloves, the fumes are **poisonous** and there is no lousier job. The acid will take away from the bright colors of the slate, and it will also eat at the grout in the cracks. You are a lot better off never using this stuff, but if you have a mess it's the only way I know to salvage it.

All right, now you've cleaned it up one way or another, the grout joints are good and hard and you're ready to put on sealer over the grout as well as the slate. Proceed as before, let it dry thoroughly and do it again, and again, and again. By this time you should have a gleaming, beautiful, magnificent slate floor. If you have an old English sheep dog like ours, it will be his favorite spot in the whole house. You'll never have to wax the floor after it's sealed, and your wife will think you're marvelous.

Now, here again are the tools you will need to install your own slate floor:

A circular electric handsaw and stone-cutting blade, **or**
    hacksaw and carborundum blade
⅛″ sawtooth trowel

Dry grout
Mastic
Slate
Underlayment board
Underlayment nails
Steel wool
One helpful wife

Natalie's Notes

I'll buy the bit about Wally being descended from a long line of "muleheaded people," which probably accounts for his frequent tackling of jobs he knows positively nothing about. But then, what better way is there to learn? How he comes out so often smelling like a rose makes me suspect there must be some Irish in his blood. Putting down the slate floor in our entrance hall is a perfect example. How the end result turned out so well after the mess we made of the grout, I'll never know. Wally also has this aggravating quality of generating such unbridled enthusiasm in projects that are against my better judgment, I'm following him like he's some Pied Piper. In 99 44/100 percent of the instances, I'm glad I did!

11 CERAMIC TILE

Installing New Tile

I was really trapped into learning how to install ceramic tile. When we bought that monstrosity of a house in upstate New York, the previous owner included in the sale a couple of thousand tiles that had yet to be installed. Part of his sales talk was painting that great imaginary picture of how the house would look once all of this assorted material was finally in its place. Installing tile? He assured me there was no trick to it at all, and when I walked into the unfinished bathrooms in the house, all with plaster dangling, pipes exposed and floors with an inch of grime, what I really saw was gleaming ceramic-tiled walls and a slate floor!

But in many ways he was right! There is no great mystery to installing ceramic tile, and if you don't mind a medium mess and several days' hard work, you can do it as well as a professional.

Few of us ever have the opportunity to install tile on new walls in a new house, so what is probably facing you is trying to ceramic-tile a wall that has been papered, painted or paneled. But anyway, first you find a wall and put it in condition so the tiles will stay put. If the wall has been painted, it should be thoroughly washed down with a strong solution of TSP. You can buy this chemical at any good paint store, and it's the best cleaner/remover available. Its full name is trisodium phosphate, and it is one of the ingredients most commonly found in household cleansers and paint removers. It costs about 15 or 20 cents a pound and is a dry powder which you mix with water. For washing down walls to get rid of loose or scaling paint, use about two cups of TSP per gallon of hot water.

Use a sponge or a brush, and be sure to wear rubber gloves. Some of the paint may remain, but that won't matter as long as all loose and flaky particles have been removed. Let the walls dry for a couple of days; then patch all of the holes in the plaster with drywall compound. (You buy it ready-mixed in gallon cans at your paint store.) Also make sure that any loose plaster is removed and that the holes are filled flush with the rest of the wall.

An alternative method is also used if the above sounds too involved for you. You can leave the old wall as it is and cover the area you wish to tile with plywood. The best type to use is the exterior variety, because it resists moisture better than conventional interior plywood. However, if you do a good job on the tile it really won't matter; the idea is to seal the tile securely enough so that moisture will not reach the wall itself. I used the plywood in the tub area of the bathroom; in fact, I put plywood all over the walls and the ceiling too and then tiled everything. The acoustics are not very good if you sing in the shower, but it sure is easy to clean, and it looks good, too! I don't know why more people don't go ahead and tile the entire shower area of bathrooms instead of just running tile up 4' above the tub and then painting the rest of the walls and ceiling. The

To install ceramic tile you'll need rubber gloves, grout, a wide sponge, a glass cutter, a tile cutter, a notched trowel, a squeegee, adhesive, a plastic bucket and a pair of tile nippers.

steam from the shower will eventually peel the paint, and once the moisture starts working on the plaster or drywall you'll never get paint or paper to stick. As I recall, I used ⅜″ plywood for my shower because I found some in the barn. If the plywood can fit firmly against the wall, ¼″ will work just as well, but the thinner variety will have to be against a firm backing.

After you've prepared the walls one way or the other, you're ready for the tiling. You really don't need a $5,000 collection of tools for most jobs, and that includes this one. The basic tools for ceramic tiling are a tile cutter, which you can borrow or rent from a tile dealer; one medium-size sponge; a sawtooth trowel for applying mastic; a 6″-wide rubber squeegee; a pair of tile nippers, which you rent with the cutter; one glass cutter and a couple of plastic pails. Provided you borrow or rent the tile cutter and the nippers, you can get everything you need for under $5.

The next part of the job is finding the center of each section of wall that you intend to tile. The purpose of this is to give you equal-sized tile along the corners of each wall. If you are going to run the tile from the tub to the ceiling, then you must also find the horizontal center of the wall. Sounds like a big deal, doesn't it? It really isn't. The easiest way for me is to get four thumbtacks and two pieces of string. Start at one of the top corners of the wall and stick the thumbtack in so that you can tie the string on it. Then stretch the string diagonally to the far corner and repeat the thumbtack bit. Now do the same thing with the other two corners. Where the strings intersect is the center of the wall. Mark the spot, throw away the string and you're ready to begin.

You can put in your soap dish now—like I did—using a jigsaw to make the hole for it.

Next, take a level and place it horizontally on the wall where you have marked the center dot. Move the level until the little bubble in it centers. Now take a pencil and draw a line on the wall, using the level as a sort of ruler—making sure the line you draw intersects the dot that marks the center of the wall. Your first tile must be centered over the dot; and the pencil line you drew is your guide for laying the first row of tiles. Take a couple of tiles and carefully apply mastic directly to the backs. The first tile goes over the dot; the next one goes right beside it. These are the two keys to a good job, because all the other tiles will now follow the pattern established.

Now apply the mastic to the wall with your notched trowel. I use a trowel with notches ⅛″ deep, which tends to leave just the right amount of mastic on the wall. A thicker coat of mastic tends to ooze through the cracks

1   2

1 In this new shower stall in our home I used exterior plywood to first
   line the shower stall. Next, I used an electric jigsaw to cut an opening for the recessed soap dish.

2 How I hate this part of the job! Ceramic-tile mastic is really a mess
   to work with. Using a notched trowel, spread it over the surface you
   wish to tile. Since it takes several hours for the mastic to set up, you
   can do a relatively large area.

between tiles and hampers the grout job considerably. Provided the wall is not as large as a football field, you can apply the mastic to the entire area before setting up additional tiles. You will have to apply the mastic carefully around the two tiles already on the wall. The mastic is the gooiest, stickiest stuff anywhere, so try to keep it off of everything except the walls.

Once the wall is covered with mastic, grab a handful of tiles and start to slap them on. Of course, you should start by placing tiles next to the ones you put up first. You can go up, down and sideways as long as you make sure you are lining up each tile with the one next to it.

Unless you are very lucky, you'll discover that the tiles will have to be cut along the edge of the bathtub, in the corners and along the ceiling. Before you start cutting, put up all the whole tiles that will fit without cutting, even going around faucets, shower heads and soap dishes. The easiest cut to make in tile is along a straight line, and your tile cutter does that beautifully. Leave about a ⅛" gap between the bottom edge of the tile and the rim of the bathtub.

Measure the gap between the last row of tiles and the edge of the tub. If the gap measures 2", subtract ⅛" and cut the tile 1⅞". The tile cutter has a 6" ruler built on, and by loosening a thumbscrew you can set a guide for cutting the tile to any desired width. Set the guide at 1⅞", score the tile with the built-in glass cutter and then apply downward pressure and the tile will break along the scored line. Have the tile dealer demonstrate the use of the cutter before you take it home. It is not complicated to use, and even a child has the strength to operate it. Take the tile and put it in place; then measure the next and continue accordingly.

Since not all bathtubs are level, you may find some vari-

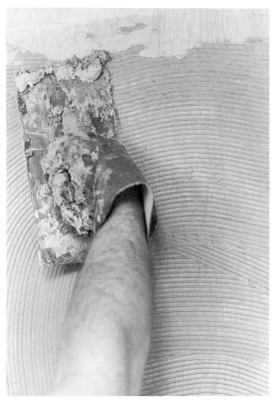

1   2

1 Please note that the notched trowel will leave exactly the right amount of mastic on the wall. Notched trowels come in various sizes, so consult with your tile dealer about which one to buy. Too much mastic will ooze through to the tile surface and be a mess to clean off. Too little mastic will result in loose tiles.

2 For a perfect job, you should install the tile so that each border tile is the same size. Find the exact center of the wall you are going to tile. Do this by stretching a string or chalk line diagonally from corner to corner, then one between the other corners. Where the lines intersect is the exact center of the wall. Simply press the tiles into the mastic. Note that each tile has built-in spacers to allow for a grout joint.

3 Straight cuts are easy to make. Just measure the width of the tile needed.

4 Draw the glass cutter over the tile, leaving a score line on the glazed surface. The type of tile cutter I am using here has a built-in ruler which can be set for the desired width. The front part of the tile cutter is a self-contained glass cutter.

5 Next, push the tile-cutter handle in a downward direction and the tile will break along the scored line.

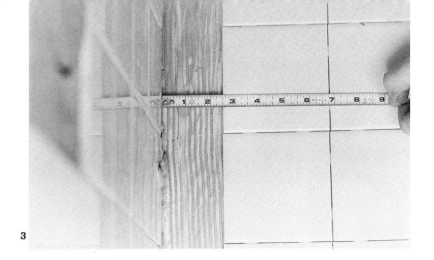

3

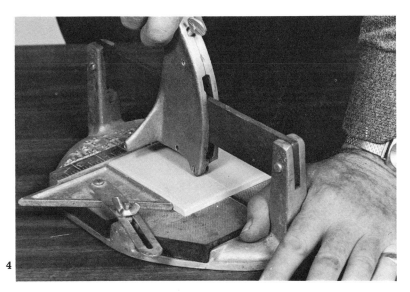

4

5

127

1

2

1 A perfect cut. It only takes about ten seconds to cut each tile after you've cut a few. I don't bother to even smooth the cut edges unless they're very jagged.

2 A cut tile such as the one in this corner should always have the freshly cut edge in the corner, the factory edge next to the adjacent tile. (Please note that because of my rush to get this picture, the grout joints on the two walls do not meet exactly. This is not desirable, but the world won't end because of it.)

ance as you progress tile after tile. This is unavoidable. The main thing is, don't let the gap between the tub and the last piece of tile exceed ⅛″. The corners of the wall and where the wall joins the ceiling are measured and cut similarly to the way you cut the tile along the tub. When you cut a tile the edge is somewhat jagged, and if you're a real perfectionist you may want to smooth the cut edge a bit by rubbing it against an emery stone before applying the tile to the wall. Remember that grout will cover a lot of minor blemishes that you may have from cutting tile, and frankly, I wouldn't bother with the emery-stone operation.

The most difficult job of tiling is notching out the tiles that fit around the various faucets, handles, shower heads and other interruptions in the surface. There is no real easy way to do it, and you may as well know from the start that you are going to waste a few tiles on your first attempt. Use a crayon and draw on the face of the tile the area that must be removed for the tile to fit around the protuberance. Then take your glass cutter and score the tile along the drawn line. Now the ticklish part. Take your tile nippers, which look like a pair of pliers, and slowly nip away at the tile, breaking off small hunks at a time. If you try to take too big a bite with the nippers you'll lose the tile, so do it gradually and slowly. Nip just enough so that the tile sort of crumbles away. The glass-cutter mark on the tile will tend to stop the crumbling, and if you nip patiently the results will be fine. You'll probably ruin a few tiles learning the technique, but it will still be a lot less expensive than hiring someone else to do it.

If you tile the ceiling of the shower stall, proceed as you did on the walls. The mastic has great holding power, and you don't have to worry about the tiles coming down like raindrops.

O.K.—you now have all the tile up and you're thinking it

Use a glass cutter to score along the lines that you have traced on the tile. Make sure the cutter penetrates the glazed surface. You can tell this penetration by a grating sound and also by the white score line.

Use a pair of tile nippers to slowly eat away small parts of the tile within the scored area. You'll break a few tiles learning the technique, but keep at it. The nippers are similar to pliers except that the jaws are sharp and slightly offset.

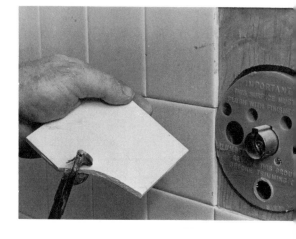

An easier cut to make is the one shown here. Again the nippers do the job if you bite off just little chunks at a time. When you try to go too fast, the tile may break someplace other than where you want it to.

looks pretty good! Before you go downstairs to have a drink to celebrate, remove all the excess mastic from the face of the tiles and clean out the mastic that has bubbled up through the cracks between the tiles. You can buy a mastic solvent that aids this job quite a bit, but the best way is to use a pointed stick or an ice pick to clean the joints. If some of the mastic does dry on the face of the tile, you can carefully scrape it off with a regular razor-blade kind of scraper. Let the tile set up in the mastic for at least twenty-four hours before you attempt to grout.

I think grouting was the easiest part of the job, but it was the part I feared the most. I've read a number of books on how to do this sort of thing, and all of them left some unanswered questions that really scared me. For example, some books describe what to do and how to do it with wet grout; others talk about dry grout. Some books said to soak the tiles with water before applying the grout; other books didn't even mention it. Here's the way I do it; it works, and it will last. Buy a powder grout from the tile store. You can get either gray or white mix. Follow the instructions on the package for mixing with water. Get the lumps stirred out of it. Now, take your sponge and a pail of clear water and slosh the water over the face of the tile. I don't know how much good this does, but that's the way I did it! After you've been over the entire tile surface, go ahead and put on the grout. With a rubber glove on your right hand, dip that hand into the grout mixture and smear it on the face of the tile. Then with the rubber squeegee, wipe the face of the tile and distribute the grout into all the joints. You can put quite a bit of pressure on the squeegee, and you'll find that a little bit of grout goes a long way. By the way, you should also put a piece of plastic in the bottom of the bathtub to catch the excess grout that falls from the tiles. You can wash the excess down the drain, but it might clog

1

1 Take a break for about twenty-four hours and let the mastic harden before you start to grout. Grout is a white powder that you mix with water and use to fill the cracks between the tiles. I smear it on with my hand, but you should really use a rubber glove.

2 Use a rubber-bladed squeegee to wipe the excess grout from the face of the tile. The squeegee will also help pack the grout into the cracks. I follow this step by wiping the tile surface with a damp wide sponge. The harder you wipe along the grout joint the narrower it will become. Next, let the grout harden (several hours), then wipe the white powdery film from the tile surface with a soft cloth.

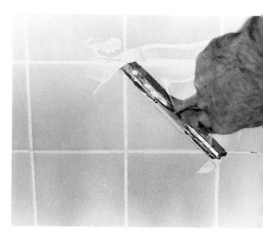

2

up in the pipe. It's better to let the grout fall on a sheet of plastic and have your wife carry it out to the garbage can.

Go over the entire tile surface with the squeegee-grout combination. Don't bother to apply the grout along the bottom edge where the tile meets the tub. After you've filled all the joints, rinse out the sponge and give it a couple of squeezes, then wipe down the tile thoroughly with its flat surface. Don't rub the edges of the sponge into the joints, but wipe each joint pretty hard. After this, accept congratulations and a kiss from your wife.

Wait another twenty-four hours, and then your wife's screams will bring you to the bathroom. Everything will be covered with a white film. The tile that looked so shiny and bright the night before is now a mess. Don't worry. Wash down the tile with sponge and water and you'll discover that the grout will not adhere to the glazed surface of the tile. Wait several more hours and then do it again. Not only will you clean the tile, but you will also give the drying grout just enough moisture to keep it from checking and popping out.

The reason you did not grout along the top edge of the tub is that the grout is an inflexible material. Most newer homes do not have a floor strong enough to keep a bathtub from moving just a bit. For example, you fill a tub with two hundred pounds of water, then your three-hundred-pound mother-in-law jumps in for a swim and the whole damn thing might end up in the basement. Usually, though, it settles only about ¼"—just enough to make the grout joints along the top of the tub crack out and look awful. Instead of grout I recommend any number of tube products that profess to serve this purpose. You'll find them in hardware or paint stores, and the rubberlike substance will dry after application but still remain rubbery. It comes in a toothpaste-type container, and you squish it into the crack just like putting toothpaste on a brush. You have to do this with a little care and steady pressure on the tube or you'll have a stringy-looking seal. The stuff isn't terribly expensive, so if you louse it up the first time you can scrape it off and do it again with another tube. Always remember, if I can do it, you can too! Take your time, use common sense and don't be afraid! Any mistakes can always be undone.

There are also many accessory-type products you may want to use when you redo your bath. Built-in soap dishes, towel racks and other items can be used in conjunction with the tile job, and none of them needs professional installation. Since the variety in this type of product is almost infinite, I suggest you obtain installation instructions from your dealer. In fact, most of these products have an installation diagram in the package. Another good rule to always follow is this: if the dealer's instructions on how to install something differ from the printed instructions in the package, disregard the dealer's advice. More often than not, the dealer or his salesman has never tried to do the job; the manufacturer has.

I hope you also realize that once you learn to work with ceramic tile there are countless jobs you can do with it. It's great for countertops, dressing tables or a children's table. It's easy to clean and comes in hundreds of colors and patterns. Even the small mosaics go on the same way as the bigger tiles; in fact, because they come glued to paper in 12″-square sheets, they are probably even easier to use. I've used tiles in a variety of ways, including applying decorator tiles to brighten up door panels on an old jelly cabinet. You can even use the decorator tiles to accent a bathroom shower. By putting them up in a random pattern, you can get very satisfying and unusual effects. Before you decide what you want to use where, go to the

tile store and look through the brochures. You'll find countless patterns and suggestions on color combinations and
style. I bet you'll really enjoy doing it yourself. I know it
will save you money!

Natalie's Notes

Can you believe that up until a few years ago I thought
"nippers" were what you called little children in England?
In my sheltered childhood, words like mastic, notched
trowels and—obviously—nippers never reached my ears.
Which is really kind of too bad when you consider how
impressed friends are when you use them in your everyday vocabulary. Thanks to Wally, the language of the paint
stores, the hardware stores and the lumberyards is no
longer Greek to me. Now, you may ask, What does all this
have to do with ceramic tiles? and I must honestly answer,
nothing. It's just that Wally has done such a good job telling you all there is to know about installing them that I
am lost for an addendum.

Replacing Tile

It really doesn't take a genius with great mechanical
talents to handle the majority of the jobs that need doing
around the average home. For example, even with my ten
thumbs I have been successful in replacing cracked and
unsightly tiles in the bathroom shower. To this day I can't
explain to you why one ceramic tile will crack and chip
away leaving the rest of the tiles shiny and gleaming, but

whatever the reason, it happens, and repairing it is no major task.

Tools required include a propane torch, chisel or putty knife, rubber gloves and a nice flat cellulose sponge. Materials include the replacement tile, a small package of dry powder grout and adhesive. If the replacement tile is a problem because of discontinued patterns, etc., you might consider using a decorator-type tile—patterned or contrasting—to replace the one that has broken. In fact, you might buy two or three of the decorator tiles and place them strategically in the wall or floor to have a more balanced effect.

The first thing you do is remove the old tile. Tiles on walls, like in a shower stall or around the bathtub, are most generally glued to the wall with a heavy mastic. To loosen the mastic and remove the tile I find it easiest to apply heat. The propane torch serves this purpose nicely, and you can buy the whole works for under $5. Light the torch and apply the flame to the tile you want to remove, gradually covering its entire surface. Keep the metal tip of the torch about 2″–3″ away from the tile and let the flame play over it. In about two minutes the tile will be too hot to handle, but hot enough to remove. Take a stiff putty knife or chisel and pry it out. Be careful that you don't nick and scar the adjoining tiles when you do this. If the tile you wish to replace is cracked through the middle or a hunk is missing, that's the best place to start. If not, you may have to start in the grout joint itself. A broken tile will come out in pieces. After you have removed all parts of the tile, take the putty knife and scrape out the softened mastic.

It's elementary to point out that the cracks around the replacement tile (which are called the grout joints) should be clean of old grout. It's easy to remove with either your fingernail or the putty knife.

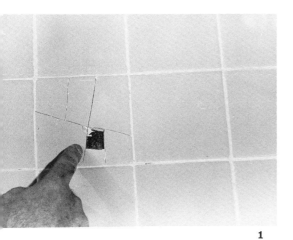

1 2

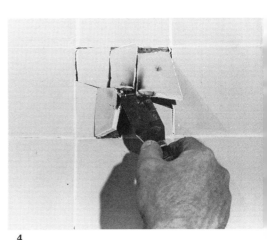

3 4

1 Broken or cracked ceramic tile in the bathroom? No big deal to replace, and anyone can do it. Modern houses are easier to work on
than older homes because in new homes a gluelike mastic is used to
stick the tiles to the wall. Older homes have the tile set in cement. In
an older home, you'll have to chip the tile out of the cement with a
chisel. For the newer homes it's much easier, as you'll see.

2 Use a butane torch to heat the tile until the mastic that holds the
tile in place softens. It usually takes about five minutes of intense
heat. Try to keep the flame from the torch on the damaged tile, because it can discolor adjoining tiles. Don't try this technique on
plastic tiles, because they will burn.

3 After heating the tile, use a stiff putty knife or chisel to loosen the
pieces of tile. If the tile won't budge, heat it some more.

4 Get one chunk out, and then use a twisting motion on the chisel to
make the other pieces come out also. Be careful, because the tile is
still hot enough to raise a blister.

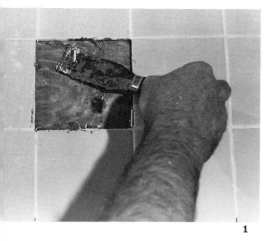

1

2

3

4

1 Use the chisel to scrape away the old mastic and particles of tile that may be sticking to the wall. Even small particles of dirt, mastic or tile will keep the replacement tile from matching the other tiles. Get all the gunk cleaned out.

2 Buy a can of ceramic-tile mastic from a tile dealer and carefully coat the back of the replacement tile with the mastic. The mastic should be about 1/8″ thick.

3 The stuff you put in the cracks is called grout. You can buy it at hardware, paint or tile stores in powder form. Follow the package directions, which usually tell you to mix it with water until you have a consistency about like mashed potatoes. Use a putty knife or your finger to fill the cracks.

4 Use a flat sponge, slightly wet, and wipe hard over the surface, including the cracks. How hard you wipe determines how much grout you leave in the cracks. Since you will be trying to match the other tiles, the width of the grout joint is predetermined. Let it dry overnight and then rinse away the white, powdery look the next day. Grout is easily removed from the glazed tile surface.

You are now ready to fill the empty space. Your hardware or tile dealer will recommend a mastic for you to use, and it's O.K. to listen to him as long as he doesn't recommend using grout as a mastic. Take your putty knife and spread a coating of the mastic on the back of the tile—about the same thickness as butter on bread. Then push the tile into place with medium pressure.

Wait overnight before you refill the grout joint, so that the mastic will have a chance to set up. Then mix the grout powder with water to the consistency of mashed potatoes. You just need a little bit—perhaps four tablespoons of powder to one tablespoon of water for the edges of one tile. Stir it well, and get rid of any lumps that may develop. Wearing a rubber glove, smear the grout mix into the grout joints, and push the mix into the joints with your finger. Don't worry about the excess grout on the surface of the tile, because it will wipe off with a wet cloth even after it is dry. After you have an ample amount of grout in the joints, take a damp sponge and wipe right over the tile, joints and everywhere else you made a mess. You'll find that the flat sponge will remove all of the excess grout while leaving just the right amount in the joints. If what you have left in the joints is wider than the other grout joints, then wipe a little harder and the new grout joint will become narrower.

It's simple! The next morning you may be shocked to see a white film over the new tile and adjoining ones. Don't worry about it, because it will wash right off.

You can replace a floor tile in the same manner, but getting the old one out is a tougher job. Ceramic floors are often set in a cement mix, and to remove one takes more than a propane torch. Hammer and chisel are best for a floor tile; but after it's removed you can put in a new one by following the same steps as for a wall tile. Remember, you can do it if you try!

12 GLAZING

I learned how to glaze windows when we were remodeling that ancient pile of stone in upstate New York, and every window, all twenty-four of them, had to be reputtied. A number of panes of glass had already fallen out of the window frames before I started the job and I'm willing to admit that I didn't know how to correct it. A couple of trips to the hardware store and asking questions of friends seemed to put me on the right track, or at least gave me enough confidence to make an attempt.

If the putty is loose and most of it has already fallen out, then chances are the little triangular points, which actually hold the glass pane into the window frame, are missing also. When the little metal points fall out, the window soon follows.

Step 1 in glazing windows is removing the old dried putty with a chisel or knife. If they really used a substance called "putty" when they put your windows in, you'll find that the stuff is almost as hard as a rock and it will take some pretty strong chiseling to remove all of it. If you find some areas where the chisel simply will not chip it out, take a propane torch and heat the old putty; then you'll find the job much easier. As you remove the putty, the

For glazing windows you'll need a good putty knife, glazing compound (which comes in paste form) and push points.

points holding the window in will probably come out with it and will have to be replaced.

In recent years they have developed a new type of glazier's point that is much easier for an amateur to use. The new type has a couple of ears sticking up, allowing you to push the point into place with a screwdriver or putty knife. Get the new type unless you're really an old pro. There is also a relatively new material on the market that replaces the old-time putty, and I recommend the new one because it is also much easier to work with. The new material is called glazing compound, and the one I have used most often is called Glazol. It's a white puttylike material, comes ready-mixed in a can and is about the consistency of modeling clay. The only other tool you'll need is a good putty knife. A good putty knife cannot be bought for 19 cents. A good one will have a strong steel blade, yet be flexible enough to bend with pressure. It will cost $2–$3, and it's worth it.

First clean out the old putty from around the edges of the glass panes. Next, push in some new glazier's points to hold the glass firmly against the wood. Now you're ready to apply the compound. The glazing compound is almost impossible to work if its temperature is under 60 degrees. If the weather outside where you're working is colder than 70 degrees, put the can of glazing material in hot water before you open it. Heat up the contents to at least room temperature before you try to press it into place with a putty knife.

In this job I use my fingers as much as I use my knife. Stick a couple of fingers into the can and pull out a glob of the compound. Roll the compound between the palms of your hands and make a rope about ½″ in diameter and about 1′ long. When you have the rope rolled, start at a top corner of the glass and gently press it against the wooden frame of the window. Now that the Glazol is in place, take your putty knife in one hand and firmly press against the wooden frame, glass and compound, simultaneously allowing the knife to bend considerably. Maintain that pressure and slowly slide the knife over the entire area to be "puttied." The more you bend the knife and the more pressure you apply, the less likely it is that the putty will tear out as you slide the knife. You'll probably have to experiment a couple of times before you get the hang of it, but it's easier to do than it sounds.

After you've finished puttying the windows, wait a couple of days and then give the new putty a coat of paint. The paint will seal the putty and keep it from drying out and breaking loose from the window. The paint permits the putty to remain flexible. Another tip: When you paint, don't worry about slopping some of the paint on the glass. After it dries, you can remove it with a razor-blade scraper.

First, scrape away the old loose putty with your putty knife and wipe away the dirt. Check the glazier's points which hold the glass into the window sash and replace or add where necessary. I like the kind of points shown because they are much easier to use.

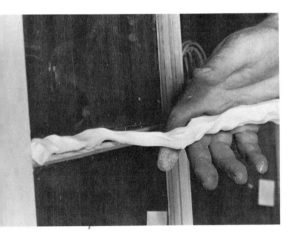

Make a rope of the glazing compound and gently press it into place in the window sash. The compound must be at a temperature of at least seventy degrees before it "works" properly.

The secret is to use a lot of pressure on the putty knife. Get a good bend in the putty-knife blade, then draw the knife over the compound.

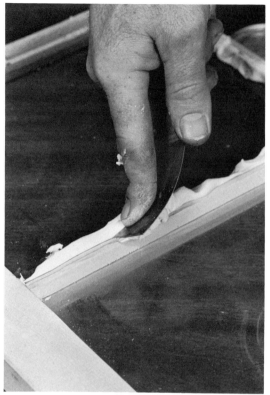

1 The excess compound will be separated from the part you want to stay on. This excess is easily removable with your fingers and can be remade into a rope for continued use. Just be sure to maintain plenty of steady pressure as you draw the knife along the compound.

2 This is one of the easier jobs, provided the compound is not too cold. Compound colder than seventy degrees will tend to crumble. After you have glazed your windows, give it a coat of paint.

1

2

13 REPLACING ELECTRICAL PLUGS AND SOCKETS

Even certain electrical repairs fall into the category of "simple." Repairing a lamp cord, for example, isn't really much more difficult than changing a light bulb. Let's start with the lamp cord.

The gizmo that plugs into the wall is usually the first thing to check, after the bulb, when you're looking for the reason why the lamp doesn't work. It can be stepped on and broken, or someone will trip over the cord and yank the wires out of the thing. Replacement plugs are available at a dozen different kinds of stores. The price ranges from 10 cents to $1, depending on the kind of replacement plug you want. Take the old plug to the store with you and buy one that looks as much like it as possible. Or buy one of the new pull-apart plugs which are usually sold in pairs (mostly because the dealer is embarrassed to get that kind of price for one) and are about 49 cents for the two. Simple directions will be printed on the package.

A few basics to remember: First, for the completely un-initiated, never cut an electrical cord until you've unplugged it from the wall, or you're in for a shocking experience! Second, it doesn't matter which wire goes to which prong when you're hooking up a new plug. Perhaps I had better say here that there are always two wires. If by some strange quirk of fate you discover more than two wires, quit while you're ahead! Most ordinary household lamps in the good old U.S.A. will have two wires in the cord, but some more expensive architectural lamps or industrial-type lamps, and perhaps some in foreign countries, may have more.

To install the new plug, take a sharp knife and sever the cord a few inches from the old plug. Then, if you're using a new pull-apart plug, pull it apart. Insert the end of the cord first into the plastic cap of the new plug, then into the hole of the other thingamajig, and squeeze the prongs together. Each prong has a metal barb which cuts through the insulation and comes in contact with the wire when you squeeze them together. Now the plastic cap slips over the thingamajig, and you're back in the lamp business. A word of advice: before you start chopping the lamp cord, make sure that your problem is something other than a burned-out bulb!

I think of what I have just described as "simple." You can get more complicated if you want, but your lamp won't burn any brighter or look any better. There are a variety of plugs available that you can use for replacement. Most of them have screw-type terminals and require a screwdriver to make the change. Again, cut the cord a few inches from the old plug. But this time, you must separate the two wires which are under the insulation before you can fasten each wire to its own place on the plug. O.K. Take your knife and score the insulation about 3″ from the end of the wire. In the case of older lamps, you'll discover that the cord has sort of a cloth covering on the outside. Remove the cloth

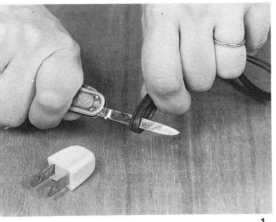

1

2

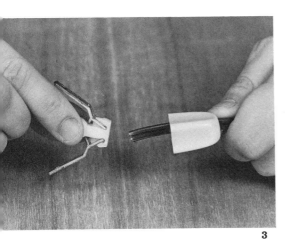

3

4

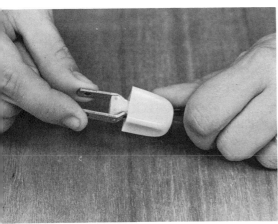

5

1 Use a sharp knife to cut off the old plug. (Make sure the old plug is **not** plugged into the wall when you do this!)
2 Thread the cord through the cap.
3 Now, open the prongs and insert the wire into the hole. It doesn't matter which wire goes to which prong.
4 Squeeze the prongs together, because this allows each prong to come in contact with a wire.
5 Now, slip the cap over the apparatus by maintaining just a slight squeezing pressure on the prongs.

or whatever, and underneath you should find two wires, each covered with a rubber-type insulation. Now, carefully remove about 1" of the rubber from each wire, measuring with your eye. You can lightly score the rubber with the knife and then, twisting the insulation between your fingers, pull it off. Anyway, get the insulation off so that you have two bare wires. Insert both wires into the hole at the top of the plug, partially unscrew the two terminals and hook one wire to one screw terminal, the other wire to the other terminal. Twist the wire halfway—or a little more— around the terminal in the direction in which the terminal will screw tight. (This is important! Otherwise the wires may not stay put.) Then tighten the terminal. Again, it doesn't matter which wire goes to which terminal.

If a fiber disk was included with your plug, you can slip the disk over the prongs and push it up against the plug. Plug it into the wall socket, and presto!—you've repaired the lamp. The same procedure will work on many household appliances that operate on 110 volts. **But,** if you don't know any more about electricity than what you've learned by reading this book, stay away from toasters, irons and other appliances that have heating elements, and certainly such things as garbage-disposal units, clothes dryers and electric ranges. Air conditioners can also be tricky, because some models are 220 volts, and this is no job for an amateur.

Lamp-socket repair is also simple, and replacement sockets are readily available at most hardware stores. (The socket is the thing that the bulb screws into.) The most common problem with sockets, particularly the pull-chain type, is a faulty switch. The easiest remedy is to replace it with a new one, and almost any replacement socket can be had for less than $1. Most lamp sockets have a threaded cap which screws onto the hardware of the lamp itself.

First, unplug the cord from the wall socket. Look care-

Separate the two wires by cutting the middle of the cord. Next, carefully remove the insulation from each of the wires. You'll want about ½″ of bare wires.

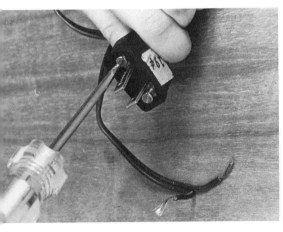

Loosen the terminal screws on the replacement plug.

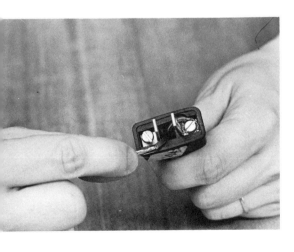

Insert the wires into the plug and attach them to the terminals as shown. It doesn't matter which wire goes to which terminal.

fully where the socket fits onto the lamp and see if there is a small set screw protruding. If there is, loosen the screw a couple of turns. Next, turn the socket counterclockwise and it will come off the lamp after five or six turns. Hold the top half of the socket in one hand, the bottom half in the other, and twisting slightly, pull apart. The electrical wires will be attached to the bottom section of the socket by two screws, one on each side. Loosen the screws, remove the wires and throw the old socket away. The new one goes on just like the old one came off. Simple? You can do it if you try!

1

2

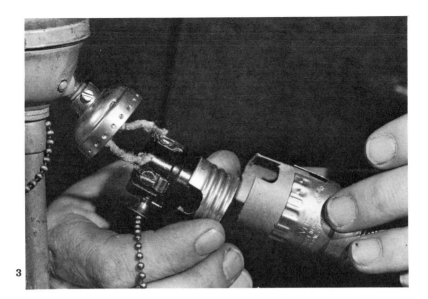

1 Most lamp sockets are held in place on the lamp by a small "set screw" like this one. Loosen the screw and the cap part of the socket will screw off.

2 Gently squeeze on the lower section of the socket and pull it away from the cap. Depressing the springlike action that holds the socket together will make it come apart.

3 Sliding the lower section of the socket completely away exposes the internal workings of the device. Two wires are attached, one to each terminal screw.

4 Loosen both wires and throw away the faulty socket. To replace the old socket with a new one, simply reverse the procedure used for dismantling.

14 LEAKY FAUCETS

Faucets are simple! They really are. A faucet usually has only one moving part, and that's about as simple as any mechanical device can be. The reason faucets leak, or drip, drip, drip, is that one part of that moving part has worn out. There is usually a combination of causes. First, a small piece of rubber called a washer has probably rotted or deteriorated after years of use. And if you live in a hard-water area, the pipes have probably corroded where the washer contacts metal and the rough edges of the metal pipe have worn the washer to the point where it no longer makes a good, tight seal. The solution is to replace the washer and get rid of the rough edges of the pipe. Don't do one without the other. A new washer will only last a few weeks if it comes into contact with rough metal edges every time you turn the water on or off.

The first step is to buy replacement washers at a hardware store. I prefer buying an assortment rather than one specific size, because the faucets in my home vary as to style and need different sizes. Besides, I can't just look at a washer in a hardware store and be sure I'm buying the right one. You get a dozen or so for 25 or 30 cents, so why not have all kinds?

After you have the washers in hand, look around in the store and inquire about a faucet reamer. This device usually sells for under $2, and it is the tool that will clean the corrosion off the valve seat so that the new washer will last for a couple of years instead of overnight. Spend the money; you're still way ahead of a plumber's house call. Besides, the reamer will last for years if you put it someplace where you can find it. You'll also need a screwdriver and a wrench or a pair of pliers, and that's all.

Before you start taking the faucet apart, you have to turn off the water supply to that faucet. Most modern homes have a turn-off valve for each faucet located under the sink or lavatory. The valve serves two purposes. It lets you turn off the water to that faucet when you want to replace the washer, and it also lets you adjust the water pressure to the faucet so that children can't splatter the whole room when they turn the water on full force. (Bet you didn't know that!) The valve handle is usually a metal disk that looks something like a small doorknob. Turn it clockwise to close, counterclockwise to open.

To replace the washer, turn the valve clockwise till it's tight. Now, turn your attention to the faucet itself and turn it on. Water will come out of the faucet at first, but should stop in a couple of seconds. If the water does not stop, you have failed to turn off the right valve.

As soon as the water stops, you are ready to begin taking the faucet apart. Different faucets come apart different ways, but what I will describe is the most common. First, remove the part of the faucet that you use to turn it off and on. This handle is usually held in place by a screw which goes down from the top of the handle into the metal stem. Sometimes the screw is covered by a little metal or ceramic disk that has "C" or "H" imprinted on it. The little disk will either pry out or unscrew. Try unscrewing it first with fingers or pliers. If it turns without loosening, you will

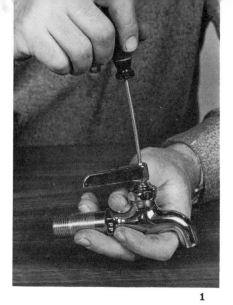

1 The most important part of changing a faucet washer is making sure you have turned off the water before you start taking the faucet apart. Look under the lavatory or sink for a small chromed valve which will turn off the supply of water. If you can't find the valve under the sink or lavatory, then turn off the main water valve where the pipe comes into the house. Next, open the faucet and relieve the pressure. When water stops coming out of the faucet, remove the screw that holds the handle.

2 You may have to pry just a bit to get the handle off the stem, but it will come off.

3 Now remove the collar or cap that holds the stem into the body of the faucet. This removal may require the use of a wrench, and it's best to first wrap the cap with adhesive tape to keep the wrench from cutting into the soft brass of the cap. The cap is threaded onto the faucet body.

4 The stem of the faucet will now thread right out of the faucet body. (The stem is in my right hand, the faucet body in my left.)

have to pry it out. I use an everyday table knife for this. Slip the blade into the small crack and twist up. Under the cap you will find the screw. Remove the screw with a screwdriver and then lift off the handle. Sometimes the handle is just a little corroded, and you might have to tap it gently to remove it. It is not threaded onto the shaft.

Now what you have is a funny-looking faucet without a handle. Next, you must remove the collar or cap that holds the whole thing together. This is threaded on. Wrap the collar protectively with adhesive tape and, using either pliers or a wrench, twist it off counterclockwise. The collar is usually chrome-plated brass and will scar easily; hence the tape. If you use pliers you're more likely to leave marks, so a wrench is preferred. Take the collar completely off and then turn the shaft or stem of the faucet counterclockwise and it will come right out. You'll find the washer attached to the bottom of the stem by one small brass screw. Remove the screw and the washer will probably fall apart into pieces if it's badly worn. If it doesn't fall out, take your fingers and pull it out. Look in your assortment of washers for one that approximates the size of the old one and put it in place and replace the screw.

Now you have to ream the valve seat of the faucet. The tool called a reamer is designed to fit into the hole where the stem came out. There are all kinds of complicated directions on the reamer package, which you may follow if you want to. If you don't want to, then listen to what I've got to say about it. All a faucet reamer does is scrape away the corrosion and burrs, which lets the washer make contact with a smooth metal surface again. The reamer is a cutter or scraper on the end of a threaded rod. Insert the thing into the hole and adjust the nut. Using downward pressure while you rotate the shaft, you can scrape the "seat" clean. That's all there is to it!

1

2

3

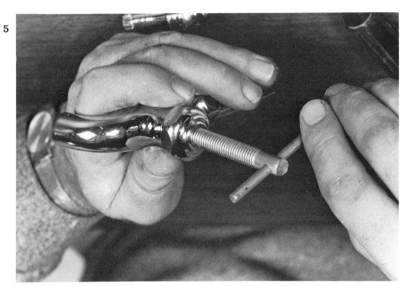

1 Now take a look at the bottom of the stem. This is where the washer is located, held in place by a brass screw. Use a screwdriver to remove the screw.

2 Washer and screw are now separated from the stem. Remove the washer from the screw and replace the washer.

3 I call this tool a seat reamer. Its purpose is to remove the corrosion inside the faucet body where the washer "seats."

4 Insert the reamer into the faucet body and adjust the knurled nut so that when the cap is screwed onto the faucet the reamer will fit tightly against the faucet seat.

5 Turn the reamer to scrape away the corrosion inside the faucet. By threading down the faucet cap, you can continue to maintain pressure on the reamer. Two or three turns are usually sufficient to do the job. Now, remove the reamer and reassemble the faucet.

Part II

INDOORS
—THE FURNISHINGS

15 REMOVING OLD FINISHES

I don't know how many times I've gone to an auction sale and seen some old piece of furniture that had interesting lines come up on the block and been reluctant to bid on it because it always seemed to have endless coats or combination thereof of what looked like paint, varnish and fifty years of grime. If you have ever had to scrape down a piece of furniture that looked like that, you know how many hours it takes. And more often than not, after you get it all scraped down it turns out to be some white wood like poplar, which was why it was painted in the first place. For years, I would just sit there at the auction and hold my hand over Natalie's mouth to keep her from bidding.

All of this happened before I discovered there are easier ways to remove old finishes than scraping them off with a knife or applying a paste-type commercial paint remover. I don't remember the piece of furniture on which I first tried a different process, but it was probably an old walnut table that I found out in the barn, all covered with varnish or something, paint and you-know-what. The garden hose got rid of most of the you-know-what, the paint was so thin that it really didn't matter, but that thick brown-looking stuff was still intact.

My furniture-stripping "kit" consists of rubber gloves, 0000-grade steel wool (not the 00 shown), alcohol, a bucket and plenty of rags.

I once read somewhere, while in the process of refinishing another piece of furniture, that everything has a solvent. Anything man can make, he can also destroy. I already knew that old furniture was never varnished by the original maker, because varnish was not discovered until the late 1800's. I also knew that the factories in my hometown never used the stuff, because varnish takes a week to dry. They always used lacquer or shellac, and still do to this day. Well, anyone who has ever used either one knows that alcohol is the natural solvent for shellac, and lacquer thinner is the solvent for lacquer. Soooooo, if the old finish on a piece of furniture is not paint, nine times out of ten it will be lacquer or shellac. Once in a while you may run into a piece of furniture that was redone in varnish by some enterprising owner, but the factory never did it that way, and not many cabinetmakers did either.

Anyway, I put the principle to work. I took that old walnut table, got a gallon of alcohol and a couple of packages of fine steel wool from the hardware store and started in. The old finish came off almost like magic! Dipping the entire steel-wool pad into one of Natalie's Haviland china bowls filled with alcohol and then rubbing briskly on the table got great results. Unfortunately, no sooner would I stop rubbing than the mess would dry right back on the table. I went upstairs and found an old chenille bedspread, tore it into strips and started in again. This time, I dipped the steel-wool pad into the alcohol, rubbed the table and wiped with the cloth, and presto!—it worked. No rubber gloves, no $5-a-gallon paint remover—just plain denatured alcohol, also known as shellac solvent.

It's a messy job: not as bad as stripping a painted piece of furniture, but still messy. Now, it's hard to tell with the eye whether an old piece of furniture has a shellac or a lacquer finish. The only way I know to do it is give it the alcohol test. If alcohol won't cut the old finish, I try lacquer thinner. If lacquer thinner doesn't do it, I mix up a solution of half thinner, half alcohol. If that won't do it, I look at the piece of furniture and try to determine whether or not it's worth the effort.

Varnish will tell you a number of things about a piece of furniture. First, if it appears to be the original finish on the furniture, then you know the piece is not old enough to be a legitimate antique. Maybe that doesn't matter to you and you want to strip it anyway because you like whatever it is about the piece that you like. O.K.: try TSP—trisodium phosphate.

You buy this chemical at your paint store or sometimes your drugstore. It comes in dry powder form and is very cheap. Mix two cups of TSP in a gallon of hot water. Add a cup of wallpaper paste to the mixture, and stir it well to

1

2

3

1 Make sure the steel wool is well saturated with alcohol before you begin your rubbing. It's better to pour the alcohol into a small bowl and dip the steel wool into it, then rub.

2 Remember, use 0000-grade steel wool, which is the finest grade available, to my knowledge. Rub with about the same pressure you use when giving a back rub. You can go against the grain of the wood without damage, but try to rub with the grain as much as possible.

3 Alcohol evaporates quickly, so you must rub the steel-wooled area with a rag, which in turn removes both the alcohol and the old finish. If you don't rub the surface with a rag, the alcohol will evaporate and the old finish will dry in a gooey mess.

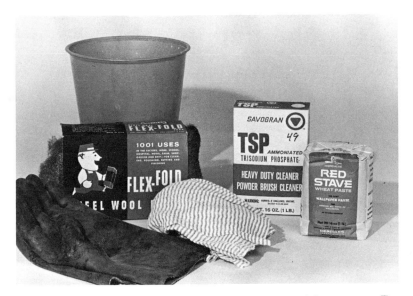

This combination makes an excellent paint or varnish remover. For flat surfaces like floors, mix one cup of TSP to one gallon of boiling water. For vertical surfaces, add wallpaper paste to thicken the same formula so that it will adhere. Good commercial paint stores sell TSP in brown-paper bags for only pennies a pound. This same formula is also great for removing calcimine paint from walls and ceiling; in fact, it's the only thing that I know of that works!

get rid of the lumps. You now have a potent paint or varnish remover of the first rank. Take an old paintbrush and apply the mixture to the surface of the great old treasure. Wearing rubber gloves, take a fairly heavy grade of steel wool, No. 1, and start to rub along the grain of the wood. It should work. If it doesn't, you can try a couple of other ideas—also keeping in mind, as the last resort, that expensive paint remover down at the store. One of the best paint removers is ammonia. Another good one is lye. Both leave some undesirable signs, but when all else fails they'll take off the paint. (They'll also take off your skin if you don't wear rubber gloves.) I'd try ammonia first.

Before you start, borrow one of those spring-type wooden clothespins from your wife and fasten it securely to your nose. Better yet, do the work outdoors, where the fumes will blow away. And make sure that what you bought is all ammonia, not some household product that says "with ammonia."

Use steel wool and a bowl, and dip the same way you did with the alcohol. Let the ammonia soak into the finish as you rub, and you'll see the finish fading away. As it breaks loose, rub it off with old rags. You'd really better wear those rubber gloves, because ammonia gets pretty hot pretty fast on bare hands.

Ammonia is particularly good for removing a large expanse of old finish, like on a floor. We had wide-plank pine floors in our old house that had a thick, black, gooey-looking finish on them which had to be removed. Ammonia was about the only thing that would do it, and even though it will darken the wood slightly with its chemical action, it's better than sanding that kind of floor and losing the age marks. Natalie worked for weeks on her hands and knees with ammonia and steel wool and didn't even wear rubber gloves! My skin is very sensitive to ammonia, so I had to be a sissy. We also found that it helps to have an electric fan turned on, so that the fumes disperse quicker; you'll find out that ammonia fumes can really take your breath away.

On floors and even on some furniture, you may find after you've stripped off the shellac or varnish or paint that there are still residues of stain left in the wood. Or if you have used a harsh chemical like ammonia, the wood may be just a little darker than you prefer. In either case, I use regular household bleach. Any liquid bleach will work fine, and the best part of all is that it will not bleach the wood any lighter than the wood is naturally. First, if you've used ammonia, give the wood time—twenty-four hours or more—to dry **thoroughly.** Then apply the bleach full strength, and let it stand on the wood for about one minute. I put it on floors with an old rag mop, give it about sixty seconds, then mop it up. You can leave it on longer if you want to, but it does about all it's going to do in a minute or so. That old mop will disintegrate in a couple of hours, and if you squeeze the mop by hand, do it with rubber gloves on. Let the floor dry thoroughly before you proceed to stain or varnish or whatever—and by thoroughly I mean at least a couple of days; even better, a week.

Use lye only as a last resort! The only time I really had to use the "last resort" was on an old walnut washstand that Natalie bought from an antique store in Ohio when we were returning home from a funeral. (I mention that simply because one should always take advantage of every opportunity to pick up a piece of furniture.) Anyway, the washstand had at least eight layers of paint. In fact, the acorn pulls on the drawers had been painted so many times it was hard to tell that one of them was missing! In my opinion, lye is the only thing to use on something like that.

First of all, do the job outdoors in a place where you don't care if the grass grows or not, because it won't! Put on the oldest clothes you have, and make sure you're wearing long sleeves and have **good** rubber gloves. Get an old bucket that you can throw away after you finish, and don't use aluminum. If it's a standard three-gallon bucket, fill it three-fourths full of water, and heat it almost to a boil. Take it outside and carefully pour in a couple of cans of lye. I say carefully because once the lye hits the water it will boil like a witches' brew. Slowly add a couple of cups of wallpaper paste to thicken the mixture so that it will adhere longer to the vertical surfaces of the furniture. Stir well but carefully.

Now you need something else you'll never use again: an old, old paintbrush. Carefully brush the lye mixture on the furniture, and make sure that every part of the table, chair or washstand is lyed. Leave the thing alone now for about ten minutes, and then get out the garden hose, stand back and wash it off. You'll be amazed at the results! Sometimes, if the paint layer was extra thick, you may have to give it a second application of the lye mixture. There will still be small areas where you will have to scrape a bit, but it's better than any other way I've tried in a really drastic situation. Let me caution you again not to let the lye come in contact with your skin. Every time I do this, a couple of drops of the stuff end up on my arms or my face, and believe me, it burns like heck. It will blister about the same way a cigarette burn blisters, and just as quickly. The bad part of the lye remover is that it will darken the wood, and it will scuff up the wood fibers. I never use sandpaper when I refinish, so I recommend steel wool to take away the roughness before you proceed to finish it however you will.

I know that many of you will disregard my home remedies for removing old finishes and still prefer to use the commercial paint removers that are available at almost every store. Fine! If I'm doing a small job, I would do the same thing. But if you're tackling the restoration of an old house and you have to strip 10,000 square feet of wide-plank pine floors, it gets very expensive at $4 or $5 a gallon! Even if you choose not to use alcohol as a remover, it still helps you determine the age of a possible antique if you know the background of finishes. Besides, I find it gets a little boring using the same junk every time I refinish a piece of furniture, and by using alcohol one time, lacquer thinner the next and occasionally ammonia or lye, I get a little variety. Sound crazy? You're right, it does! But anyone who goes out and buys an old piece of junk and starts stripping fifty years of paint has to be a little crazy to begin with. I qualify; how about you?

16 STAINING, SHELLACKING, VARNISHING

Now that your monstrosity has been stripped and peeled, steel-wooled and pampered, what do you do with it? Well, it depends on what you want and what you like. If there is some confusion in your mind about what to do with it, don't worry, your wife will decide for you if she is like mine.

I have a couple of rules about acquiring antiques. Number one, I never intentionally buy something that I don't like. A couple of times, of course, this has not worked out. Like the time I bid on a horse-drawn buggy and found myself writing a check because no one else opened their mouth. Or when the carved dolphin-base table that I foolishly thought would sell for $150 was knocked down to me at one-third the price.

But seriously, I try to determine the age of a piece and what kind of wood it is made of before I ever open my mouth at an auction. This takes a little practice, and even today I may make a mistake once in a while, but what I am trying to say is that I won't buy something if I can't make it look better than when it's sold, or unless it is already in perfect condition and needs nothing done.

I lean heavily to pieces made of solid cherry, walnut, mahogany or pine. I have several eighteenth-century English antiques which are veneered, but with rare exceptions such as this, I do not stray from that pattern. My favorite wood is walnut, and with the right finish I believe it to be the most beautiful of all woods. I prefer the natural wood color as opposed to messing it up with stains, and I also really see no purpose in staining cherry or mahogany, ever. Pine is something else, but the hardwoods have great graining and configurations which I think are better left alone. What you do depends, again, on what you or your wife want. In this area I rule the roost in our house, and this is the way I do it and the way I recommend it to be done. Don't put me down until you hear my whole story!

After you have stripped the piece of furniture, scraped all of the gunk out of the cracks and crevices and steel-wooled it until it's satin-smooth, you're ready to apply the finish. I use shellac. Don't laugh. I remember as a kid when I was forced to take woodworking in school how we always put a thick coat of shellac on everything we made and it looked like it came from a carnival. Maybe I flunked out of the course before I found out what to do next, I don't remember, or more likely the instructor in the course didn't know there was another very important step. Regardless, I use shellac on the finest antiques I own and they turn out looking magnificent—in my humble opinion.

First the basics. When you finish any kind of wood, be it with paint, varnish or one of the new plastic finishes, you must first seal the wood so that the final finish does not penetrate into the wood fibers. The only time you won't use a sealer is when you are going to put on an oil finish—which I think is foolish, but my sister swears by it. Anyway, buy a quart can or bottle of white shellac and a quart of alcohol. For the first coat on any piece of furniture use a half-and-half combination of shellac and alcohol. A cup of shellac mixed with a cup of alcohol will cover the world, so unless you are sealing something bigger than that, that's all you will need. Because alcohol evaporates quickly, you won't be able to store what is left over, so throw away what you don't use. Get a 2″ or 3″ brush (this time a new one) and smear the sealer on. You don't have to be very careful, and because the mixture is so thin, it will run and puddle. No problem. It is best if you try to get it on as smoothly as possible, but you don't have to worry about some runs.

Fifteen minutes after the mixture is applied it will feel almost dry, unless it's a very humid day. In that case you shouldn't be doing it anyway, because shellac, like other finishes, just doesn't set up right when the weather is wrong. Shellac, for example, is anhydrous (water-sensitive), and excessive moisture in the air will make shellac turn white as it dries. Don't try to apply any finish in a damp basement or during a heavy rain. Even if the finish is not anhydrous it will take forever to dry, and this increases the number of dust particles and other foreign matter that will stick to the tacky surface.

Wait a couple of hours and make sure the shellac is dry. (I hate that kind of direction in books I've read. How do you make sure it's dry? You feel it with your hands. If it doesn't feel tacky and you can run your hand over the surface without getting stuck, it's dry! O.K.?)

Now, get the finest grade of steel wool you can buy. Depending on where you go, it might range anywhere from 00 grade to 0000. The finer the better. Work with the grain, and try to rub off the shellac. No, I'm not crazy! The more you rub the more white powder you'll get, and you'll notice

1   2

1 After the finish is removed, you're ready for a sealer coat of white shellac, thinned 50–50 with denatured alcohol. Don't use orange shellac for this sealer coat, and make sure you use half alcohol, half shellac.

2 I use a 2″ or 3″ paintbrush to apply the shellac. Try to avoid serious runs and streaks, but don't worry about it if they develop. The mixture is very thin and will be dry to the touch in ten or fifteen minutes.

that suddenly the surface is becoming almost satin-smooth. Rub about as hard as you rub the baby's back when you're trying to get him to go to sleep. The shellac you're removing is all surplus. You made the mixture thin so it would penetrate the wood, and what's left over is what couldn't get in. Take it off, take it all off, and then do it again. That's right. Give it another coat of the same mixture, let it dry and again remove it with steel wool. It's easier than it sounds, and the results are really worth the effort.

Usually I quit at this point because I have the kind of finish that I want. I'll give the piece of furniture three or four thin coats of paste wax and put it in the living room until Natalie comes home and puts it where she wants it. If the piece that I'm redoing happens to be a table, I take one more step.

Shellac is not a very serviceable surface for tabletops. Since its natural solvent is alcohol, one drink glass will leave a magnificent ring. Even a glass of water will damage it, because the anhydrous qualities of shellac will result in a white ring. So before I wax, I give the top a couple of coats of polyurethane. Some paint dealers call the stuff polyurethane varnish; others just call it polyurethane. Don't ask me why. Still, make sure it is polyurethane. You can brush it on without thinning it, and it won't get bubbles or streaks like the old varnishes. Apply it carefully under good light and leave it alone until it dries completely. (Same test on dryness as for shellac.) Again use fine steel wool and rub lightly until the surface is smooth. Unlike the case with the shellac rubbing, don't try to remove all of the polyurethane; just rub until you get the little bumps out of the surface.

The directions with most polyurethanes say give the second coat within twenty-four hours. O.K., do it. And

1

2

1 Wait a couple of hours after shellacking before you steel-wool the
finish. Again use 0000-grade steel
wool, removing as much of the shellac as you can. About all you want
left on the furniture is the shellac
that penetrated the wood and works
as a sealer. Be sure to remove all of
the gloss. (Much easier than stripping.)

2 After steel-wooling, give the chair
a thin coat of paste wax. Then, over
the next couple of weeks, wax it
every other day, buffing in between.
It will glow beautifully!

after the second coat, go over it again with steel wool and get rid of any roughness there might be on the surface. Polyurethane is available in several different ranges of gloss. You can buy high gloss, satin gloss and dull gloss. I like the satin because it more closely matches the waxed look. If you use the high gloss and it comes out too shiny for your taste, you can always steel-wool the surface until you have the degree of gloss that you like.

Now remember, I don't believe it is necessary to do the entire table in polyurethane—only the top. Why go to all of the trouble to do the whole thing when it isn't necessary? If you have kids who climb table legs maybe you should do everything in polyurethane, but in most cases, why bother?

Now, back to shellac. Maybe you won't like the look of the piece of furniture after you've shellacked it, steel-wooled it and waxed it. (You have bad taste.) Don't decide you don't like it after you've waxed it, decide before! Wax is tough to remove. Mineral spirits will do it better than anything else I know of, but it's awfully hard to get every speck of wax off a piece of furniture, and of course nothing else will go on top of wax and last very long. At this point (before the wax), you can still go in several directions. You can paint it. (Ugh.) You can varnish it, but that won't change the color or appearance unless you want to add color to the varnish. If you do that—add color—it will tend to darken the finish, and you will be concealing the grain of the wood. I can't imagine anyone not liking the shellac finish, but if you're really unhappy with it, get rid of it! You do that by removing the shellac with steel wool and alcohol, and you're right back with a piece of stripped furniture. Let me warn you! Unless the wood is walnut, cherry or mahogany or some exotic wood, you won't like the natural finish that shellac gives you. If you want to see how a piece of wood will look with a natural shellac finish, throw a bucket of water on it and you'll have the same effect. If you're neater than that, or if your wife objects to your throwing a bucket of water in the house, take a wet rag and wipe it over the surface of a stripped piece of furniture. That's how it will look; that's the color it will have, plus a little more gloss. Darker woods look great this way, but light woods like pine, poplar, maple or beech might not be to your liking.

On the lighter woods, you may want to use stain—**before** the shellac is applied as a sealer. Just in case you're a real amateur at this, let me explain that once you use shellac on wood, you can't stain the wood unless you first remove the shellac. Why? The shellac seals the wood and will not let anything else penetrate the surface. Stain has to penetrate to work; therefore, no penetration and nothing happens.

What color do you stain the wood? You have to experiment. A good paint dealer has an infinite variety of stains already packaged and ready to use. He also has samples showing how the stain affects various woods and what the end results looks like. If none of the prepared colors suits you, he can mix a stain of your choice.

I generally use an oil-base stain and usually have it mixed at the store. I have learned the colors I like by doing it, and I won't begin to imagine that any two people will necessarily like the same combinations. For example, we stained those old wide-plank pine floors in our house with a color called Antique Cherry. Since the cherry stain was a little too brown for my taste, I had the paint store add H-8 to it. "H" is the code letter for a certain shade of red, and "8" is the amount of that color. It gave a reddish cast to the finished color, and I have since used that color stain on wood paneling and other things as well. You have to experiment a bit, and also remember, walnut stain on pine will look different from walnut stain on maple.

Decide on the color; then apply the stain to whatever it is you're staining. I do it with an old rag. I get out another bowl from Natalie's kitchen, pour a little stain into it and dip the rag, and away we go. My hands have been more colors than the rainbow because I never have rubber gloves around when I want them. It's best to use gloves. (Your paint dealer has disposable vinyl gloves for a dime or so.) Rub the stain-soaked rag over the surface of the wood. Let the rag be fairly juicy with stain, but try to get at least a halfway even coat as you go. The longer you leave the stain on the wood, the deeper the penetration and the darker the color. Most stains will give you their medium color in five to ten minutes, and this is the color you saw on the sample in the store. Take a clean rag and wipe off all of the stain that did not penetrate the wood. You can rub it as hard as you like, but don't wait until the stain gets tacky before you start. After you've wiped and rubbed, let it dry. (Same test as before.) Twelve hours is not too long to wait!

All right, the surface may feel just a little rough, and you may want to lightly steel-wool the wood before you go ahead. Don't press excessively hard or you'll create light spots in the stain. Remember, the reason the surface of the wood feels rough is that the penetration of the stain raised some of the wood fibers. All you're doing when you lightly steel-wool this time is getting rid of the fuzz on the surface.

After the piece is dry, you can give it the water treatment to see if you'll like what you've done. Don't go overboard on the amount of water you use: simply wipe a moist cloth over the stained surface and take a look at it. If it appears to be too dark, get out the bleach. If it's too light, give it

I'm amazed how many people do not know how to stain! Use rubber gloves. Pour the stain onto a piece of toweling—or, better, pour a little into a bowl—and saturate the rag.

Rub the stain-soaked rag over the surface you want stained, making sure you have a reasonably even coating.

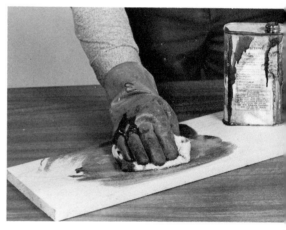

To get the full color of the stain, let it remain on the surface for at least five minutes. Then take a clean piece of toweling and wipe away the stain that has not penetrated the wood.

another coat of stain. If it's just right, let the wet area dry and give it the shellac treatment.

Chances are that the instructions on any can of varnish you buy will recommend anything but shellac as a sealer. If I made varnish, I might do the same thing. Don't worry about it! Shellac works fine under varnish, polyurethane, paint, etc. Besides, it's cheap!

I would like to put to rest in this chapter a couple of things that have been bugging me for a long time. First, don't use the stuff they call spar varnish on anything that is going to spend its life inside the house, because it never really dries. Spar varnish is for out-of-doors only—for things like the exterior side of doors, boats, and that sort of a job. I don't know why any amateur would ever use anything but polyurethane if he wants a varnishlike effect. Polyurethane is better as a protective coating, it's easier to apply and while it may cost a little more than the old varnishes, what's a couple of bucks on a family heirloom?

Some folks, including my sister, are big on a linseed-oil finish. It's easy to do if you want to do it the rest of your life. For a real linseed-oil finish you strip the furniture according to my instructions, then start rubbing on linseed oil, a thin coat at a time. That's all! Every couple of weeks you can give it another coat, then another, and another and another. Eventually the wood will turn almost black from repeated oilings and the collection of dust between layers of oil. Linseed oil almost never completely dries. It isn't really tacky, it's oily, and that kind of surface will attract dust very readily. It will look fine until it gets too dark, and there really isn't much you can do when that happens. I don't really know of any way to get rid of a linseed-oil finish, and I believe you can have a nicer piece of furniture with the shellac treatment.

But shellac isn't the only finish you can use—it's just the

1 Even though many stains also claim to be sealers, I use a coat of white shellac over the stained area. This guarantees a good seal and also serves as a good primer coat for regular varnish or polyurethane.

2 Let the shellac dry completely; then use a very fine grade of steel wool to remove the roughness and high gloss. If you're working on a bookcase or something similar, you can quit. If it's a tabletop or a piece of furniture that may have considerable use, give it a couple of coats of polyurethane in addition to the shellac.

easiest! If you want to invest in fairly decent spray equipment you may want to use lacquer, as most of the furniture factories do today. Lacquer dries in seconds, cannot be brushed satisfactorily, but looks great. It can be shiny, satin or dull. It can be clear or colored, and it does give a tougher finish than shellac. The spray equipment will probably cost under $100, and in some areas can be rented. You need a place to spray and you have to learn the technique. It's easy to correct mistakes because you can always wipe the lacquer off with lacquer thinner. If you plan on redoing a heap of furniture, like everything in your mother-in-law's house, get a spray outfit and use lacquer as your finish. If you're a now-and-then refinisher like me, stick to shellac (No pun intended).

Let me make something else perfectly plain. As I stated in the introduction to this book, there are twenty ways to do every job. I'm telling you a few of them and about the ones that I have come to prefer as the result of trial and error. You can get fancier than me if you want to! I once worked in a furniture factory, and I assure you that I have no desire to be a professional furniture refinisher. There are all sorts of aniline dyes, some used with alcohol, others with water, that can be employed in refinishing furniture. I guess I figure that if you wanted a really professional job on an original Chippendale highboy you wouldn't be reading this book. I find it fun to occasionally work on something with my hands. I'm not that fancy, but I get pretty good results.

Natalie's Notes

There's no getting around it: stripping furniture or floors is probably the messiest and most tedious work you can find. So I have two bits of advice for those of you who are positive that an invaluable antique lies beneath those umpteen coats of shellac, varnish, paint or whatever.

First, find out if there is someone in your community who refinishes furniture at a reasonable price. If not, and unfortunately this is usually the case, do it yourself, but do it outdoors. Spring and fall are the best seasons. Have lots and lots of extra rags available, and think happy thoughts.

For those of you who have never worked with stains, I strongly recommend experimenting with a piece of wood very similar or identical to the object you are planning to stain. Some types of wood, such as pine, absorb stains very quickly, so you won't want to wait very long before wiping it off. Remember, you can always make the stain a little darker, but you're asking for a lot of unnecessary work if you stain something too dark initially. I know; I've done it.

Along with Wally, I prefer a shellac finish. I really don't know why one has to put on so many coats of shellac only to rub them off, but I do know I like the end result.

17 ANTIQUING

Talk about a misnomer! If you really want to antique a piece of furniture, you can't do it with a paintbrush! But still, every year millions of "antiquing kits" are sold, and everyone, including myself, tries to antique furniture.

To really antique a new piece of unfinished furniture, you should rub it down with a rusty tire chain, flick some ink spots on it from an old-fashioned fountain pen, make some wormholes with a darning needle and then let it sit outside in the weather for a couple of months. That's antiquing! But no one believes me when I tell them that's the way it should be done. If you really want to antique a piece of furniture, you have to do it that way; if you want an unusual finish on a piece of furniture, you can do it with a paintbrush.

The art of using a paintbrush to get an unusual or so-called "antique" finish probably originated with craftsmen who wanted to make a piece of pine furniture look like mahogany. This was a common practice with doors and woodwork in older homes. They called their technique "graining," and the tools they used ranged from wooden or horn combs to the tail feathers from turkeys and roosters! To achieve their end, they used many tricks of the trade. First, they usually applied a base coat of paint, called a "ground color." Usually it was yellowish in color. This was allowed to dry. Then over the top of the base coat they used a variety of other colors, each painstakingly applied to simulate the grain of the wood they were trying to fake. In woods like mahogany and walnut there was usually a black streak in the grain. In clearer woods like maple or cherry they were not after contrast so much as uniformity of the grain. This is the basic concept of the antiquing kit that is most often sold in stores today.

First you apply a base coat which completely obliterates the true surface or grain of the wood. You then apply the "glaze" coat, which is a streakylike finish, and then over the top of that you apply a varnishlike finish. Frankly, I cannot call that an antique finish! It can be an interesting finish, a pretty finish, an unusual finish, but antique? No! You want to do it anyway? O.K., I'll tell you how.

Any piece of furniture that you are going to "antique" must **first be sanded**! Not a lot, but at least a little. Even a new piece of unfinished furniture should be lightly sanded before you apply a sealer of shellac. Even if the piece of furniture already has a coat of something-or-other on it, it should also be gone over with sandpaper, which roughs up the surface and makes the first coat of paint stick better. I don't think it is mandatory to completely strip a piece of furniture prior to giving it the antique treatment. Make sure all the flaky pieces of the old finish have been removed, sand it a bit and you're ready for Step 1. There are a variety of base colors you can successfully apply to a piece of furniture. In fact, use any color you want. The glazes, or streaks, also come in several different colors, and you should use the one that best contrasts or harmonizes with the base color. The final coat, or finish, is usually "clear," but there are no hard-and-fast rules on this either, and a pigmented varnish or shellac can be used. I simply wish to point out that there are many options open to anyone who wants to use a little of their own ingenuity to redo an old whatever-it-is for whatever reason. This is the way I do it, and it will give you the basics. Add any variation you want to.

If I'm working with a new piece of furniture, I first sand it lightly, then give it a sealer coat of shellac diluted half-and-half with denatured alcohol. I brush the shellac-alcohol mixture on the piece of furniture, wait about thirty minutes for it to dry, then go over the piece with steel wool until the surface is smooth. If the directions on the paint can say, "Don't use shellac as a sealer," ignore them!

Next, I give the piece of furniture the base coat of paint —the color coat. Again, brush it on carefully, then let it dry. (It will probably take about twelve hours.) After the base coat has dried, use either fine steel wool or fine sandpaper and go over it lightly. (Just sort of knock off the rough edges and bumps.) Now give it a second application of the base coat, let it dry and again go over it lightly with either sandpaper or steel wool.

Next comes the glaze! This is the stuff that gives you a streaky appearance. You can get this look with a variety of tools, including a paintbrush. The glaze is designed to be streaky anyway, so it doesn't really need much help. You can paint it on and it'll look streaky! You can try to get fancy by using an old sponge, dipping it into the glaze, then pressing it on the piece of furniture. Strangely enough, the resulting pattern will look like one made by an old sponge—but who knows, maybe that's what you had in mind. You can still buy graining combs at paint stores, and if you have access to a turkey tail feather maybe you'll want to try that! I also on occasion use a piece of cloth and

1

2

3

4

1 Step 1 for me is to thoroughly sand the piece of furniture, then give it a coat of shellac. I use a mixture of half white shellac and half denatured alcohol. This thin mixture will dry completely in about thirty minutes. The shellac mixture seals the wood.

2 After the shellac has dried, steel-wool the piece of furniture until it is smooth and slick. Fine-grade steel wool will remove the high gloss and roughness.

3 Use a 2″-wide paintbrush to apply the ground color of the antique kit. The first coat will probably look streaky when it dries. After the second coat the streaks will disappear.

4 After the second coat of ground color, again use fine-grade steel wool to remove the roughness. Just lightly steel-wool—don't try to "dig in."

1

2

3

1 The glaze coat is the one that gives you the streaky effect, or so-called antique look. You can brush it on, or use a variety of different-textured materials for different effects. You can dab it with a sponge, smear it on with burlap, etc.

2 Do every part of the piece of furniture, even the underside. The leg turnings can be streaked either vertically or horizontally depending on your taste.

3 It takes a couple of days, counting drying time, for the finished result. It's worth the time, and I believe you'll enjoy the result.

gently smear the glaze coat on. In my opinion, the glaze looks better if it is not applied in a uniform manner all over the piece of furniture. A little heavier in some areas than others, a little lighter glaze coat where normal wear might occur, all add up to a more interesting result. Now, I'll admit I've seen some rather horrible examples of furniture that people have "antiqued." You can't believe what some people do to a piece of wood. The only saving grace is their pride in accomplishment. Just recently Natalie and I were guests of another couple in their home. I don't know what they did to an old desk, but it was the most God-awful-looking thing I'd ever seen. They asked me what I thought of it and I responded with something like "It's very interesting," but what made it all work out was the great satisfaction the couple had working together to create this monstrosity. It might have saved their marriage!

Don't worry about what someone else is going to think about it. Do it to your own satisfaction and enjoy it. I'm sure that some people who come to our house must cringe when they see a lot of ball-and-claw Chippendale. I don't care! The important thing is that **we** like it. So go to it!

Natalie's Notes

I must agree with Wally that there are, unfortunately, too many pieces of furniture ruined by overzealous "antiquers." But I will also readily admit that I have seen some lovely effects achieved by this technique. For instance, the painted and grained woodwork in our 125-year-old house in upstate New York was so beautifully executed it was almost impossible to distinguish it from "real" wood.

Frankly, I would limit "antiqued" furniture in my home to the kitchen, rec room or children's rooms. But as Wally says, when it comes to taste in furniture (and women), "To each his own."

18 SIMPLE UPHOLSTERING —AND REUPHOLSTERING

Cornice Boards

I guess I did my first upholstering when I worked at a furniture store in Oklahoma City that specialized in making draperies, cornice boards and lambrequins. To this day Natalie insists that there isn't any such thing as a lambrequin, but as I recall, the store I worked for made a lot of them and got some pretty fancy prices, too. What a lambrequin really is is a fancy cornice board, upholstered and custom-made for fancy windows. Call them what you may, they are relatively simple to make, and you won't need a furniture-factory workshop to do the job.

I guess the nicest thing about lambrequins, or cornice boards, is that you can make one that will fit almost any style decor from Early American to French Provincial. When I was a network correspondent in the U.S. Senate, I always admired the elaborate lambrequins that decorated Senator Everett Dirksen's office. They were, of course, in the Federal period, and they were of immense size, appearing to be almost 3′ in height. They were gold in color and covered matching gold draperies.

As I recall, we had a rule of thumb in making these things so that they would be in proportion to the height of the room. For example, you couldn't use a 3′-high lambrequin in a room with an 8′ ceiling. If my recollection is correct, we used to figure the height of cornices by allowing 12″ plus one-twelfth the height of the room. So for an 8′ ceiling the lambrequin should be 20″. But again, there is no hard-and-fast rule to follow; it's simply a matter of taste. More probably a matter of your wife's taste, since women tend to become just a little bossy when you start messing around with windows, curtains and draperies. Let her decide how big the things should be and I'll tell you how to make them.

You'll need a handsaw, a hammer, a few nails, a roll of cotton batting (the kind used for quilting), a staple gun, several hundred straight pins and lining material. You will also need a sufficient quantity of drapery material, which can either match or contrast with the draperies. The cornice itself is constructed out of 1″ x 3″ pine boards, and for the face board we used ⅛″ beaverboard.

The first thing you do is measure the outside dimension of the window where you intend to use the lambrequin. Measure from the outside of the woodwork to the outside of the woodwork, and allow an additional ½″. By this time your wife should have decided how tall the cornices will be. Construct a simple wooden frame, making sure that the **inside** measurements of the frame are equal to the overall measurement of the window. Remember, the cornice fits on the outside of the woodwork, not on its face.

Take one piece of one-by-three for across the top; then cut two shorter lengths, one for each side leg. In each case, allow for the thickness of the pine board. For example, if the window is 40″ wide, the top board will measure 42½″ long. If the height of the cornice is going to be 18″, and you nail the sidepieces under the top board, the sidepieces will measure 17″. Make the frame so that the completed cornice will jut out 3″ from the wall. In other words, don't make the sort of frame that will fit against the wall and not permit enough room inside for the draperies.

After you have nailed the three wooden parts of the frame together, you are ready to staple the beaverboard to the frame. At this point, measure the outside dimensions of the frame. For example, the cornice board we have been talking about would measure 42½″ x 18″. Cut the beaverboard with a sharp knife to those dimensions. Place the piece of beaverboard (or any ⅛″-thick material) on the frame and staple it in place. Now it's design time, and this is the most fun.

You can put any type of scroll pattern you want across the bottom edge of the board. I like to take brown wrapping paper the length of the entire cornice, fold it in half and with scissors try a variety of patterns before I decide. The reason you fold the paper in half is to make the pattern symmetrical when you open the paper and trace it on the cornice board. If you're short on ideas, get a book that shows pictures of homes furnished similarly to yours. You can copy a Chippendale scroll, or a Queen Anne curve, or even the up-and-down Oriental-type decoration.

After you've decided on a pattern, trace it along the bottom edge of the beaverboard and, with a sharp knife— razor-blade or linoleum type—cut the pattern. This is best done on a table, with the beaverboard turned so that it lies face down.

The next step is to attach the cotton batting to the entire cornice board, giving it the upholstered look. I generally use a double thickness of the batting and cover all parts

Step 1 on a cornice board is making a wooden frame. I use pine boards, 1″ x 3″. Measure the window from one outside edge of the woodwork to the other. This will determine the horizontal dimension. If you want the cornice to extend away from the wall more than 3″, use wider boards. The height of the board is a minimum of 12″, or personal taste.

You'll have a neater-looking job if you trim the edges of the legs. This trimming will make the entire cornice appear to be more "delicate."

I try to use ⅛″ beaverboard for the cornice face. This pressed-paper material is easy to cut, yet rigid enough to upholster. Plywood ¼″ thick will also work. If you use plywood you'll have to nail it to the frame. Beaverboard, shown here, can be attached with a staple gun.

SIMPLE UPHOLSTERING—AND REUPHOLSTERING   **193**

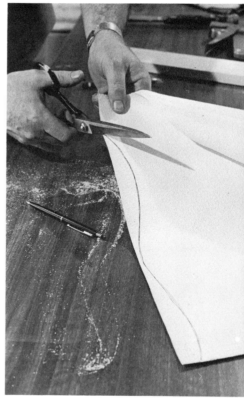

1

2

1 I call them lambrequins, Natalie says they're cornice boards. Anyway, make a pattern for the scrolled edge. Measure a piece of paper the size of the cornice board. Fold the paper together, and trace the pattern along the edge.

2 Keep the paper folded and cut along your pencil line.

3 Open the folded paper and you have a pattern for the scroll edge of the cornice.

of the outside of the cornice board. Along the lower edge you can cut the cotton to correspond with the pattern. Put a few staples into the cotton simply to hold it in place.

The next step is applying the drapery fabric. If you have nice, wide material the job is a lot simpler, because you will not have to sew two pieces of fabric together in a matched pattern. For example, material 48″ wide will not have to be pieced on this cornice board that we are making. Material 36″ wide would have to be. If the material has no pattern you have again simplified the job, because you will not have to worry about vertical lines and it isn't nearly so important to keep the material perfectly straight.

With a pattern, you must use the straight-pin method for keeping the material straight and tight. With patterned material you should start at what will be the top edge of the face board when the cornice is hanging on the wall. Place the cornice board on a table face side up and place the drapery material over the cotton. Starting with the top edge, insert straight pins about every inch through the drapery material and cotton and into the beaverboard. Make sure the pattern remains straight and that all vertical and horizontal lines are just that. You don't want the material so tight that you can bounce a quarter off the finished fabric; I think "snug" is the best word to describe the degree of tautness you're after.

After you've pinned along the top edge, stick a few pins along the sides just to keep the fabric snug. Then stick a few pins along the bottom edge, and now, alternating as you go, make what looks like a pincushion out of the edge of the entire cornice board. Once all the pins are in place, flip the board over so that the drapery material is face down on the table. Gently pull on the remaining material, ease it over the edge of the 3″ frame and staple it on the inside of the frame. When you get to the corners, you'll

1 Trace the paper pattern onto the beaverboard or plywood. Beaverboard can be cut with a knife. If you use plywood, you'll need an electric jigsaw.

2 Use cotton batting for the upholstered look. Place the cornice board face down on two layers of cotton and spot-staple it (just a couple of staples here and there) in place.

3 Next, place the drapery material, pattern side down, on a table. Then place the cornice board covered with cotton on top of the fabric and trim the fabric to the approximate size of the board.

1

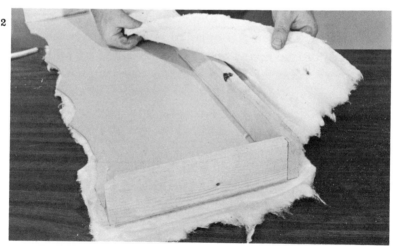

2

3

have to notch and trim the material just a bit to remove the bulk of folded-over fabric. By this I mean cut away any excess material so that you will get a smooth corner. Continue to staple the material to the frame along both sides and the top edge.

Now all that's left is to finish the patterned or scrolled edge. Trim the fabric so that no more than 2″ of material extends past the edge of the cornice board. Now, if the lower edge has a scroll pattern, take scissors and every 2″ make a cut within ¼″ of the edge of the pattern. After the cuts are made, staple each 2″ strip to the back of the beaverboard so that you can hold the snugness of the fabric. The cuts allow you to compensate for the uneven edge and will prevent the material from puckering and pleating as you fold it over. If the edge is straight, just staple it up.

Even though you can't really see up inside the cornice board, lining it makes the job look more finished and professional. Drapery-lining material is usually a white faille which is simply stapled to the inside of the cornice board to cover the rough edges.

All you have to do now is mount a bracket on the inside of each end to hold the rod that will hold the draperies. To mount the cornice board on the window frame, use two or three metal L's called angle irons, which you can get at a hardware store. The L-shaped piece of steel looks like half a picture frame. Two screws hold it to the woodwork; two more screws go into the top board of the cornice board. Beautiful? You bet!

Natalie's Notes

Wally's right! You can achieve a professional-looking job in your own home. I'd suggest getting your husband

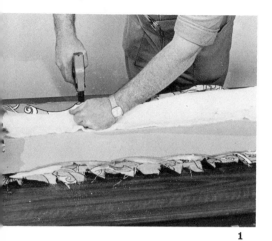

1

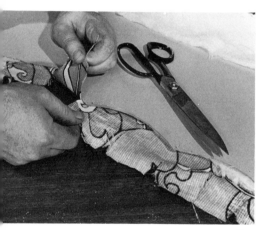

3   4

1 Use a staple gun to attach the material to the cornice board. Start at the top edge, being careful to keep the welt of the fabric straight as you staple. Remember, you want the material snug, but not stretched overly tight.

2 Fold the material around the corners of the board and staple in place. Remember to try to conceal the folds in the material as much as possible. You can do this by pulling the material tight and keeping the folded-over part of the fabric away from the front of the cornice.

3 Do the front bottom edge last (along the scroll). You'll have to snip the material almost to the edge of the cornice to eliminate the "puckers."

4 There you are: the finished whatever-it-is! It takes about one hour for the first one, thirty minutes or so for each one after that.

(or boyfriend) to make the frame while you play the "designing" woman.

By the way, Wally, a lambrequin is not a "fancy cornice board," etc. According to Mr. Webster, a lambrequin is a "curtain or drapery" covering the upper part of a window. What you have just given instructions for making is a cornice board—in spite of what they may call it in Oklahoma City!

Reupholstering Chair Seats

The simplest of all reupholstery jobs is the pop-out-type chair seats or the seats and backs of dinette chairs.

Natalie bought twelve Chippendale-style chairs at an auction, and the original mohair fabric on all the seats needed replacing. The seats in the chairs were the pop-out, or insert, type, removable after you take four screws out of the frame.

If you turn this type of chair upside down and take a look at the bottom of the seat, you'll see a hole in each corner, and if you look closely into the depths of the hole you'll see a screwhead. With a screwdriver, remove the screws, and with just a little pressure the seat will pop out! Our chair seats also had webbing and horsehair padding, and since they were a couple of hundred years old, this needed replacing as well.

Remove all materials from the chair seat—fabric, stuffing and webbing—and you'll find a wooden frame similar to a picture frame. After you have ripped all the material off the wooden frame, make sure you remove all of the old nails, tacks and staples that may have remained in the wood.

Your next stop is an upholstery shop where you can buy webbing, foam padding and materials for a new seat. Natalie looked everywhere for a simulated-needlepoint seat for our chairs and finally compromised on a medallion design that falls somewhat short of the original thing. For antiques, needlepoint seats are just magnificent, but taking the time to make the needlepoint was her problem, and probably yours too! Unless you are a real purist about restoring antiques, throw away the old rubberized hair stuffing that you removed from the seats and replace it with one of the new plastic or rubber-foam-type materials. The webbing that you replace should be about the same size as the original, and you'll need a webbing stretcher, which you can buy at a good hardware store. The stretcher has a wooden handle like that of a paint scraper, and one end has ten or twelve short protruding points, which you use to grip the new webbing for stretching. The only other tools you'll need are a staple gun and a pair of scissors. Stretch the webbing in a lattice pattern and, pulling tight with the stretcher, staple the ends to the wooden frame. Next, place the piece of foam padding on the frame and trim the foam so that it extends about ¼″ beyond the sides of the frame. Place your new upholstery material pattern side down on a table, and then place the seat on top of that. If you have a medallion-type pattern, you will want to be most particular in positioning the pattern in the center of the chair seat.

Once you have the pattern where you want it, you are ready to fasten the fabric to the underside of the frame. Start along one edge and with the staple gun attach the fabric to the frame every 2″–3″. Move to the opposite side

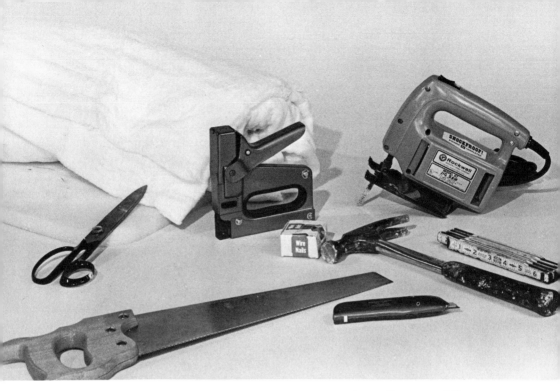

Reupholstery equipment: scissors, staple gun, wire nails, saw, utility knife, hammer, rule and electric jigsaw.

and apply pressure downward on the seat as you fasten the other side. You want to compress the foam just enough so that the finished seat will have a "taut" appearance. Now do the other two sides and you've finished.

It is difficult to give a universal description of how to do this sort of thing, because the type of fabric you use can cause variations. For example, if you're using a stretchy-type material you cannot complete one entire side without getting puckers when the fabric is stretched in the opposite direction. In this case you should begin with one staple in the center of each side of the frame, being careful that you apply the right tension as you do this. Then carefully work your way around the frame from those points one staple at a time, taking up the slack in the material as you go. After the fabric has been securely fastened, trim off the excess.

Most women I know, my wife included, would like to

take one more step at this point, that of applying a dust cover on the bottom of the seat. I always argue that anyone who goes around in my house looking under chair seats isn't welcome, but Natalie insists that it must be done.

For some reason, most upholsterers use a thin black material for places like underneath seats. Why not? Get some kind of cheap, gauzelike black material and cut the fabric to the same size as the bottom of the chair seat. Attach the black fabric with your staple gun by stapling through the material into the wooden frame of the chair seat. When the seat is placed on the chair, the edges of the black material, along with the staples, will be hidden by the chair frame itself. Stretch the material as tight as possible when stapling. Now when your guests turn a chair upside down they won't see all the ragged edges.

An even simpler job is redoing the seats of chrome-type dinette chairs. These are usually covered with some sort of plastic or vinyl, and it isn't unusual for the covering to split or peel after a couple of years of use. Four screws hold these seats in place too. Turn the chair upside down and look at the bottom and you'll see what I mean. Remove the four screws and the seat will slip off. Cover right over the old material if you want to, because this type of seat does not require the webbing that is a part of the other type of chair. If you want additional padding on the seat, add a piece of foam rubber, then the new fabric, and with your staple gun attach the fabric to the underside of the seat. Dust covers are no problem here either, because the underside of the seat is usually a piece of plywood or hardboard.

The two simple tasks I have described are really designed to help you get your feet wet in reupholstery. Once you have done one or the other, you may be tempted to tackle some other upholstery problem around the house. Go to it!

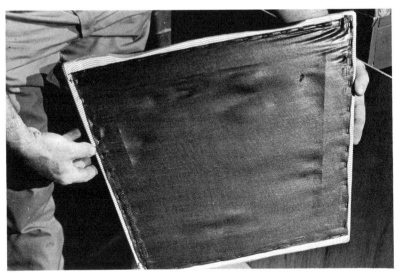

The top photo shows the finished upholstering job on a "pop-out"-type seat. The bottom photo shows the dust cover installed on the underside of the seat. This also hides the ragged edges of the upholstery fabric and makes for a much neater job. To install the dust cover, simply staple through the material.

Natalie's Notes

Yeah, well, you can give 'em all that gung-ho "You can do it if you try" pep-talk type of stuff—but nobody, but nobody but a professional upholsterer is going to touch any piece of furniture larger than a dining-room chair in my house!

It is relatively simple, though, to redo dining-room and kitchen chairs. I know. I've watched. Just be patient—particularly around the edges, where heavy or stretchy-type materials can cause gaping problems. Actually, I'm not really as fussy as Wally makes me out to be, but I do believe that if you're going to take the time and effort to do something, you should do it right. On second thought, maybe I am that fussy.

1

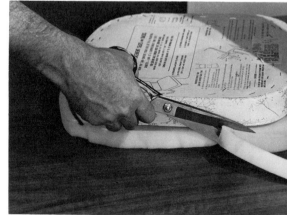

2

5

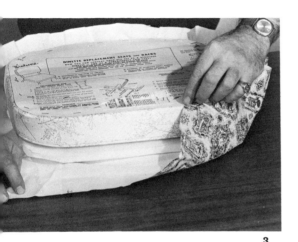

3
4

1 This is a regular dinette chair seat, which you can easily remove from the chair frame by turning the chair upside down and removing four screws.

2 Leave the old covering in place and install new padding on top of it. In this case I'm using plastic foam; cotton will also work. Trim the padding to approximately the size of the seat.

3 Next, place the new fabric face (pattern side) down and trim it so that you have just enough to fold over to the underside of the seat.

4 Tacks and a hammer will work just as well, but a staple gun makes the job easier and faster. Stretch the material tight, and staple through the fabric into the underside of the seat. Staple or tack about every 2″ around the perimeter of the seat.

5 The more patience you have, the nicer the corners will look. If you're not particular, just fold the material over the corner and staple. You'll have some "gathers" which will show. If you carefully slit the fabric you can eliminate the folds at the corner, but it's a bit tricky for an amateur.

19 PICTURE FRAMING, MATTING, GLASS CUTTING

Most people find the simple tasks difficult when they try to do them in an impossible way. For example, a miter box is a basic and necessary tool anytime you're going to cut wood for picture frames, unless you have an excellent table saw that will make mitered cuts in wood.

Let's start with a miter box. There are a variety of them on the market, and the prices range from $5 to $100. If you take your time, the $5 one will serve as well as the expensive variety, and it's the one I use with quite a bit of success. You'll also need a fine-toothed saw, which will cost another $5–$6. Also essential for making frames is a corner vise, which sells for less than $2 at my hardware store. So for less than $15 you can buy all the tools you'll need to successfully make picture frames. You can of course spend more money if you want to, but there is really no reason for it.

If you have ever paid to have a picture matted and framed, you know how expensive it is—which is probably

Equipment for picture framing and matting: miter box and saw, sand-paper, white glue, rubber cement, glass cutter, utility knife, corner vise, rule, wire brads, glazier's push points and a framing square.

why you're reading this chapter. Anyway, let's assume you're trying to save money by doing it yourself.

Lumberyards have an infinite variety of standard mold-ings which are easily adaptable for frames. The lumber people will call them cove moldings, doorstop, crown, etc., but take a look at them before you go to a frame store, because they cost less than frame moldings. Remember, too, that you can combine a number of lumberyard mold-ings and make a really sensational-looking frame for a fraction of what you would pay for a ready-made one.

Making your own frame also allows you to use any kind of finish you want. You can paint, stain, varnish or antique it to blend more harmoniously into the decor of your home.

To make frames, you must first learn how to make a miter cut in a piece of wood. The inexpensive miter box has a built-in gauge that allows it to be adjusted for a variety of cuts. You can set the gauge for 30 degrees, 45 degrees, 60 degrees and 90 degrees. In picture framing, a mitered corner is 45 degrees. By setting the gauge, inserting the material to be cut against the frame of the miter box, then carefully sawing within the metal guides, you'll get a perfect miter every time. I find it advisable to carefully sand the fresh cut just enough to remove the "fuzz" before putting two cuts together in the corner vise. Eliminating the fuzz will give you a neater fit, and the miter cut itself will be less noticeable and therefore more attractive.

A picture frame will require four pieces of wood cut on the miter, and the two directly opposite sides of the frame must be the same length for the frame to square and for the corners to fit properly. For example, let's say you're going to make a frame 10″ x 12″. The two 10″ pieces must be exactly the same length, and so must the two 12″ pieces. A deviation of even as little as ⅛″ will result in an open gap at one of the corners.

After you have made the mitered cuts, the next step is to assemble the frame with small finishing nails, or wire brads, and glue. It's a near-impossible task without the $2 corner vise, but with the vise it's very simple. The vise is designed to hold two pieces of wood simultaneously at a right angle, which gives you the corner you need. Insert the two pieces of wood into the vise, spread white glue on the edges where they are to be joined, slide the two pieces together and tighten the adjustment screws to hold them in place. Drive in a 1″ nail (smaller for very narrow moldings) so that it penetrates both pieces of wood. Remove the vise and proceed to the other corners and repeat the process until all four corners have been done. Lay the frame aside overnight or until the glue has completely

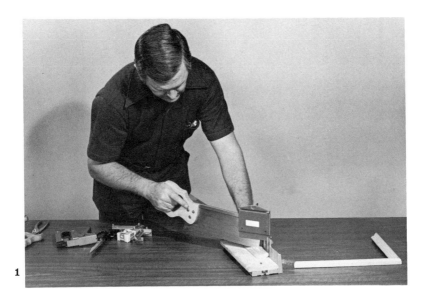

1 Select your picture-frame molding from the lumberyard or hardware store. Make the inside measurements of the frame 4″ larger than the print you are going to put into it. (It's really a matter of personal choice.) Adjust the miter box to a 45-degree angle and carefully cut the molding to size.

2 Notice how the guide of the miter box holds the saw in place so that you get a nice clean angle.

dried. Don't skip the gluing operation! Glue makes the only permanent joint between two pieces of wood. They might build houses with only nails, but picture frames will not stay together very long without the glue. The little nail in each corner of the frame is only used to hold the frame together until the glue dries.

Many picture frames require a piece of glass to protect the print or picture you're framing. You can buy glass at most hardware stores already cut to your specifications, and if you're only going to make one frame, let the store do the cutting to size. However, if you're making several frames you can save money by cutting the glass yourself, since most stores have a minimum price for glass, regardless of the size piece you want.

Glass cutting is another easy job that most people haven't tried because they don't know where to begin. A glass cutter is a small hand tool that costs less than $1. You'll also need a straightedge, preferably metal, and something to measure with. That's it.

Place the piece of glass you want to cut on a piece of cardboard. Measure the size piece you need and draw a line on the glass with colored crayon or grease pencil. Take a metal straightedge and holding it firmly against the surface of the glass, draw the glass cutter along the marked line so that it "scores" the surface of the glass. As you draw the glass cutter over the glass you should hear a grating sound, and you should also be leaving a white etchlike mark cut by the tool. Make sure that the pressure you apply as you move the glass cutter is even and that the mark on the glass is uniform. Now turn the entire pane of glass over and, using the opposite end of the glass cutter (usually a wooden handle), tap along the score mark and the glass will break cleanly along the line!

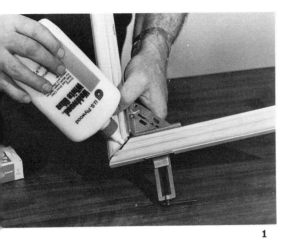

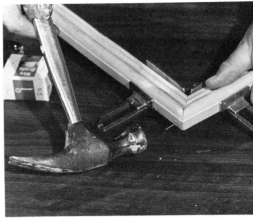

1

2

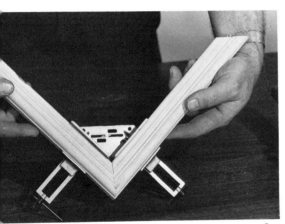

3

4

1 Next, place two legs of the frame into the corner vise and run a bead of glue where the two legs join.

2 Slide the two legs together and tighten the vise so that it holds the section of frame in place. Now drive a 1″ wire brad into the corner of the frame.

3 It's best to let the glue dry before removing the vise, but after you have nailed the frame you can remove it if you're in a hurry and do the other section of the frame.

4 One way you get a nice, neat corner like this is to carefully sand the saw cut of the miter before assembling the frame. Don't sand hard; just touch up the saw cut and remove the wood fuzz.

Now you're ready to cut the glass to fit the frame. Use a scrap of matte board or cardboard to work on. You'll need the framing square as a straightedge, plus a glass cutter. Measure the inside of the frame to determine the size of the glass. Place the glass on the cardboard, hold the straightedge firmly in position and score the piece of glass with the glass cutter. Apply considerable pressure when you draw the glass cutter over the glass. A grating sound will tell you you're doing it the right way.

After you have scored the glass, turn it over so that the score line is underneath. Now, use the glass cutter to tap along the line until the glass breaks.

Hopefully, it will break like this one did. Once in a while it won't. Make sure the score line is continuous from one edge to the other. Most problems in glass cutting occur when the score line is not deep enough or when you do not draw the score line completely from edge to edge.

The next step is to fasten the glass within the frame by using glazier's points (see page 141). Put the frame on a table face down, drop in the glass (gently), put four points on the glass itself and one by one push them into the wooden frame with a screwdriver, one point into the middle of each side of the frame. The glass is in place and now you're ready to cut the matte board.

There are many ways to make a matte board, but I believe I have found the easiest way of all. I use three pieces of board to start with. Pieces No. 1 and No. 2 are cut to the same size—the inside dimension of the frame; in other words, the same size as the glass. To cut the board, I use a regular razor-blade knife. I make a third piece of board the exact same size as the picture portion of the picture I wish to matte. Next, I take board No. 3 and position it on board No. 1 so that I have it either centered, if I so desire, or at least positioned in what I think is the most attractive way to display the picture. I hold board No. 3 in place and then carefully, lightly trace around its edges. After you have traced around board No. 3, remove it, and with the razor-blade knife carefully cut out that section that you have marked on board No. 1.

Now you can check to see how the picture will look before you make the installation permanent. Place board No. 1 over board No. 2. Board No. 1 is going to be the front —the matte; No. 2 will be the backing. Slip the picture in between the two boards and line it up so that it all fits. Remove the picture and board No. 1. Apply a coat of rubber cement to board No. 2 and press the picture in place. The positioning doesn't have to be exact, because the rubber cement will allow you to move the picture just enough so that it will line up with the other board. Now, place board No. 1 over the picture. I usually put rubber cement on board No. 1 also, but it isn't essential. Slide the picture around

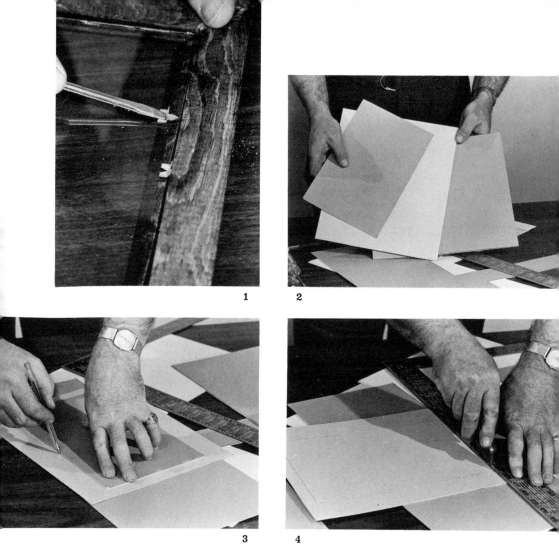

1   2

3   4

1 Push points like these are easy for the amateur to use and work
  beautifully. They're called glazier's points. After the glass is placed
  in the frame, simply push the points into the wooden frame with
  either a screwdriver or a putty knife.

2 Now for the matting. I use three pieces of matte board when mounting a picture. First, measure the exact size of the "picture portion"
  of the picture you are going to frame. Make a cutout that size. Then,
  cut two more pieces of matte board the exact size of the inside of
  the frame.

3 Take the piece of matte board that will in fact be the matte that you
  see on the finished framing job and trace the picture size on the
  board with a pencil.

4 With the framing square as a straightedge, use a utility or razor-
  blade knife to cut out the inside section of the matte board.

3

1

2

1 Carefully trim into the corners after you have removed the cutout section of the matte.

2 I use rubber cement on the back of the prints that I mount on matte board. Give the back of the print a liberal coating of cement, then place it on the backing board. Next, give the matte board itself the rubber-cement treatment and place it over the picture. Rubber cement does not dry immediately and you can slide the print to position it perfectly with the matte board.

3 Stain or paint the frame and you'll have something like this. A framing shop would probably charge $20 for this sort of job. You can do it for a fraction of that price, including buying the tools you'll need.

until it is perfectly framed in the matte-board opening, and now insert both boards and picture into the frame. Easy? You bet!—and it looks great this way.

Natalie's Notes

Now, this is something I can do, and it's not only fun but a great outlet for one's "creative" impulses.

You'd be amazed at the selection of moldings available at lumberyards. You can create the most elaborate frame imaginable by putting together various types of moldings —page 215 shows a Wally Bruner original—or opt for a simpler style, probably most desirable for photographs.

My only comment on the above is a suggestion to those who never knew miter boxes existed. Before you ruin a piece of frame, try out the box on an extra piece of framing or the end of the piece you will be using. And, as W. B. always cautions me, "Measure twice, cut once."

Oh, yes: don't panic when you place your "invaluable" print on a matte board covered with rubber cement. At some later date, you can detach it without ruining the print.

Who knows, making a picture frame might even bring out the Picasso in you. And what nicer gift is there than an original picture—and frame?

20 DÉCOUPAGE

This is a fun thing to do, and pronouncing "découpage" is more difficult than doing the job! I'm certain that purists in the field of découpage will cringe when they discover how I simplify the process, even though the end result meets with my satisfaction. What I believe découpage to be is the art of applying pictures, scrolls or other decorations to pieces of furniture or wood plaques so that they are permanently mounted and will not be damaged by the average household routine (booze glasses, for example).

Some very fancy découpage kits are available on the market, and I'm sure they will produce a high degree of satisfaction. However, I prefer the home-remedy method, and I defy anyone to tell the difference between the way I do it and the way the experts recommend. It is also less expensive to do it my way, and you can get almost all of the materials needed at any paint store instead of waiting weeks for a mail-order delivery. On the television show **Wally's Workshop,** I've shown the basic steps necessary for mounting an old Currier & Ives print on a piece of wood. This same method can be used for applying a picture to a tabletop or an old chest, or even mounting the picture in a frame for an antiqued-picture look.

Let's assume you have purchased a piece of unfinished pine furniture and you want to dress it up or customize it just a bit. For the sake of explanation, let's use a small "cricket" stool as an example. This is the sort of furniture you will probably want to either stain or paint first. Decide what color you want and proceed according to the directions in the staining or antiquing chapter. If you do decide to stain the stool, let the stain dry for at least twelve hours and then give the stool a coat of white shellac, which you've thinned with an equal part of denatured alcohol. Brush this thin mixture on the stool and let it dry in a warm room for about one hour. Next, steel-wool the shellac finish until the stool looks dull. Take as much of the shellac off the surface as possible, using the finest-grade steel wool available (preferably 0000 grade). The shellac will seal the stain into the wood and prevent the stain from bleeding over the surface of the picture or decal.

If you are using an old print, I would recommend giving the back of the print a coat of the same mixture of shellac and alcohol. This is particularly important if there is printing on the back, as on a newspaper column or even an old calendar print. In fact, if the printing on the back is heavy, you should give the back of the print a coat of flat black paint before you attach the print to any other surface. The black paint will prevent the printing on the back of the picture from showing through the finished job. The shellac and paint will also stiffen the paper print so that it will adhere flatter to the surface of the piece of furniture. (If you are applying the print to a piece of furniture that you have stained and shellacked, you are now ready to fasten the print to the surface.)

Decide where you want the print; then, using a white glue, coat the entire area where the print will rest. After the glue is spread, carefully position the print on the glued

1   This circle of plywood represents the furniture surface to which you're applying a découpage. First saturate the toweling with stain and wipe an even coating over the wood.

2   Let the stain dry and then give the wood a coat of shellac to seal the stained surface. I prefer using a half-shellac, half-alcohol combination for this purpose. It will dry in about thirty minutes or less and makes the next step a shorter wait.

3   Quite often the print you want to use may also have printing on the other side. In that case, you'll have to give the underside a coat of flat black paint to keep the printing from showing through. The print I'm using here is a Currier & Ives reproduction which I found on an old calendar.

4   Brush the black paint on so you get a nice, even coat. Remember, if there is printing on the back, this step is important. Even a newspaper clipping can be painted on the back to keep the show-through from happening.

area and run your fingers over the print, gently pressing it to the surface. Next, take a 6″-wide rubber squeegee, the kind you use to clean windows, and with medium pressure draw the squeegee over the surface of the print, removing the excess glue from under the print. This also tends to flatten the print to the surface. Make sure you use enough pressure to remove all bubbles and wrinkles that might develop at this stage. Use a damp—not wet—cloth to immediately remove the excess glue from around the edges of the print and off the surface of the wood. Let the glue dry thoroughly before going on to the next step. Thoroughly means at least twelve hours in a warm room.

After the glue has dried, check the print carefully and make sure the edges of the print are securely glued to the surface. If not, add more glue where the edges are loose and wait again for it to dry.

O.K. Now you're ready for the final step. I prefer a polyurethane finish to anything else on the market. It is more resistant to alcohol, water and children. It is easy to apply with a brush and does not bubble as regular varnish sometimes does. Give the entire piece of furniture a coat of polyurethane. It will take between twelve and twenty-four hours to dry. After it has dried, gently rub down the surface with fine steel wool, then give it another coat.

You can use any one of three different types of polyurethane—very shiny, satin or dull. If you don't know what you want, you can always start off with a high-gloss finish, and if that is too shiny you can cut the gloss by rubbing the surface with steel wool. Rub carefully over the print portion that you have applied. You can, of course, use a variety of pictures and clippings to completely cover a piece of furniture. In fact, decals are available at paint stores and will work just as well as an old print. You can even buy a scroll decal for around the edges of a table. Just follow the

Next, use a good white glue in a very thin coat over the entire area to be covered by the print.

Press the print down on top of the glue and use a rubber-blade squeegee to firmly press the print against the wood and to draw off the excess glue.

The final step can go on forever if you want to spend that much time. I usually give the wood and the print two coats of satin-gloss polyurethane and call it quits. Others prefer a high-gloss finish on découpage and give as many as a dozen coats for a "built-up" look. Suit yourself.

package directions for its application, then use the polyurethane over the decal the same as if it were a print. You can use a bit of ingenuity and come up with very attractive results. Since we are antiquers, we like the old look as opposed to the Grand Rapids effect. We were able to procure several calendars from the 1940's which had reproductions of Currier & Ives prints on them. They were in very good condition, and in fact, I framed some of them just the way they were. Others I experimented with. For one, I used a pine board as the backing, cutting the board so that it was larger than the print. Then, after staining and shellacking the board, I scorched the paper print with Natalie's iron. I put the iron on the linen setting, which is the hottest, and slowly ironed the print until the originally white paper turned yellow. I also made the edges of the print ragged by carefully trimming the edges with scissors. Then I glued the print to the wood and gave it a coat of polyurethane, and the result looked like it was a hundred years old.

You can also get a découpage effect when you antique furniture with a regular antiquing kit. If you're antiquing a new unfinished piece of furniture, first give it a coat of shellac to seal the wood. Next, paint on the base color, let it dry and then add a second coat. Lightly go over the painted surface with steel wool to remove the "bumps," then glue the print to the painted surface. Let the glue dry before you add the glaze coat. The glaze coat is the finish which gives you the "lined" effect. If you are going to give the piece a heavy lined look, I would recommend that you lighten up the lines over the print. However, I suggest that a light application of the glaze is more desirable when you are using a découpage, because the antiquing should be somewhat uniform. After the glaze has dried, give the piece the polyurethane treatment. The scorched look goes very well with an antique finish, so you may want to com-

1 Another option is frayed edges. I do this sort of thing with Natalie's manicure scissors. Stiffen the paper first by pressing with a hot iron. Hold the print in one hand, the scissors in the other, then pull the print through the open jaws of the scissors and tear off just a bit of the edge with each pull.

2 This step is a matter of taste. After the paint has dried on the back, I use a regular electric iron, set on its hottest setting, to yellow the edges of the print. This also tends to stiffen the paper of the print and makes it easier to attach to the wooden surface.

bine the two! Let me remind you once more that if the print you are going to apply has printing on its back, you must give the back a coat of black paint or the printing will show through. I learned this the hard way. The old calendar prints I was using had a picture on one side and numerals on the other. The worst happened. Every number is visible because I did not give the back of the print the paint treatment.

This is the sort of thing that is fun to do. Since there are several steps involved regardless of whether you stain or paint, I always buy a half dozen cheap 2″ paintbrushes which I use once and then throw away. This takes some of the drudgery out of découpage, and since I assume you're doing it for fun, let's keep it that way!

Natalie's Notes

I've never tried the "orthodox" way of applying découpage to a surface, but I've heard my mother's friends comment on the umpteen coats of varnish they have applied to an article. So if this is indicative of the work involved in doing it the regular way, give me Wally's method any day. And there's no limit to the things a person can "découpage," from picture frames and furniture to ladies' wooden handbags and luggage. You haven't lived till you've seen a découpaged toilet seat. And as W. B. says, if you keep the process simple, there's a lot more fun in the doing.

P.S.: For those who have always wondered what the word "découpage" meant but were too lazy to look it up in the dictionary, Mr. Webster comes up with this definition: "the art, technique or method of decorating something with paper cutouts." Those of you who took French in high school may recall that **découper** means to cut out.

Part **III**

OUTDOORS

21 SLATE ROOFS

The hardest part of working on a slate roof is finding a way to keep from falling off. A couple of words of caution to begin with. Don't ever try to walk on a slate roof! Every footstep will result in broken shingles, even if you wear tennis shoes. A slate roof is very durable, weathers better than any other kind, but it is also very brittle; if you have to climb around on a slate roof, do it with a ladder laid flat against the roof so you can distribute your weight over a wide area of the surface.

When I started repairing my over-a-century-old slate roof, I bought a long length of heavy rope and tied one end to one of the chimneys and the other end around my waist. While Natalie stood anxiously on the ground, I was able to navigate on the roof in the manner of a mountain climber, and I found this solution to be most satisfactory. Be sure the chimney is sound.

Slate shingles are installed with two nails, and that is all that holds them in place. After years of service the nails may begin to rust away and the shingles can start sliding off the roof and shattering on the ground. Replacement shingles are still available from most roofing or lumber companies, and even if they do not have a shingle that is the exact size of the ones on your roof, you can cut it to size when you get it home. If you have a 6″ or 7″ electric builder's saw, you can buy a stone-cutting blade for under $4. The cutting blade has no teeth, but its abrasive action trims slate perfectly. You'll get a lot of stone dust when you saw the shingle, so wear goggles. But the sawing is easy to do. You'll also have to drill a couple of holes in the new shingle if they are not already there. Oldtime slaters made the holes with a tool called a slater's hammer which punched the holes through the slate without breaking the shingle. I think it's easier to drill a hole with an electric drill. Since the slate is usually no more than ¼″ thick, it doesn't take much effort to drill the hole, and it also keeps an inexperienced hand from shattering shingles while learning to use a slater's hammer—if indeed you had a slater's hammer. If the shingle you are going to replace is in the last row of shingles installed on the roof, then you have a relatively simple job. The last row of shingles is the one at the very peak of the roof, which is usually covered with a cap-type molding made of aluminum, copper or sometimes tin. Lift the cap enough so that you can slide the shingle into place and then drive in the nails. Replace the cap and your job is finished.

For some reason, though, the shingles along the cap seem to last longer than those right in the middle of the roof. But replacing a middle shingle is even easier, and besides, you don't have to crawl so high to do it. First, make sure all of the slate is out where the shingle appears to be missing. Sometimes a slate shingle will break and the uppermost part will remain embedded in the roof, held there by the remnants of two rusty nails. You'll have to get rid of the nails before you can work the piece of slate out of its slot. I made a tool which I found worked very well. I took an old 18″ lawn-mower blade and sharpened one end like a chisel. That gave me a homemade 18″ chisel which was thin enough to slide under the other shingles and with one good lick from a hammer sliced the old nails off even with the roof. After the nails are eliminated, work the remaining slate, if any, out of the roof and you're ready for the next step.

Most lumberyards stock copper flashing for residential use, and after you get over the shock of the price you'll be all right. In my area, copper flashing is sold by the pound and comes in long rolls. You can buy as much or as little as you want, and you also usually have a choice of from 12″ to 18″ widths. Two or three feet will help repair a lot of missing shingles from a slate roof. Measure the length of the shingles that are on your roof and buy the copper flashing accordingly.

Next, take tin snips or Swedish cutters and cut strips of the flashing about 1″ wide. Put the copper strip on a piece of wood and punch a couple of holes about 1″ apart, in line, at one end of the strip. The copper strip is going to become a bracket of sorts to hold the replacement shingle in place, since there is no way to nail the shingle as the others are nailed. Nail the copper strip into the roof by driving the nails into the crack between the two shingles already there. (Look for yourself, but there is a crack just wide enough.) Next, slide the new shingle into place right over the copper strip. With the shingle in place, you should have several inches of copper strip extending past the end of it. Carefully bend the strip right up over the shingle and trim the strip with your cutters so that only about 1″ of the strip is exposed to the eye. This copper tab will hold the shingle almost forever, and after a few weeks of weathering the bright copper will turn a dull brownish shade and you won't even be able to see it.

1

2

1 The toughest part of replacing a slate roof shingle is staying on the roof. The problem shown here, however, is a missing slate shingle in the middle of the roof. If part of the shingle is still there, it must be removed before you can install a replacement shingle. I made a chisel out of an old lawn-mower blade, and this works quite well to remove that part of the old shingle which may be jammed up in the shingle slot. Notice that a small section of the roof's wooden decking is exposed in the cracks between the shingles still in place.

2 Use either copper or aluminum flashing, and cut a strip 2″ wide and long enough to protrude past the edge of the replacement shingle. I prefer copper for this because it will tarnish to a dark color and blend in better with the roof.

1

2

3

1 Now position the copper strip over the exposed crack between the other shingles.
2 Nail through the copper into the roof decking with at least two nails.
3 Insert the replacement shingle over the copper strip and into position. Now bend up the tab of copper that is exposed to hold the new shingle in place.

22 PICNIC TABLE

I had just started what I thought would be a restful week-end when Natalie announced that we were having the neighbors over for a cookout! They are, indeed, good friends; however, even good friends will think twice before sitting on the grass to eat a steak.

I had put off buying "outside" furniture not only because it is almost unreasonably expensive, but also because much of what is available in my area is on the flimsy side. So when my dear wife announced the plans for a cookout, I decided to build a picnic table that would serve the occasion. I wanted a really heavy-duty table that would seat as many as ten people and one that would take all kinds of weather, winter and summer, and not fall apart. I had less than four hours for the entire job, so it had to be fairly simple. The results were very impressive, and the total cost was under $35!

You will need ten boards, pine or fir, 2″ thick, 12″ wide and 8′ long; one 10′ length of two-by-two and eighty-two carriage bolts, ¼″ in diameter and 3½″ long, with nuts and washers. While you're at the lumberyard, you might as well get a gallon of exterior stain, which will give the fin-

The tools required to build a picnic table include an electric drill with 5/16″ bit, electric saw, hammer, wrench and framing square.

ished table two coats with just a bit left over. I used a red-wood-color stain on my table, but there are a number of other colors available also.

The tool list to get the job done is also simple. An electric handsaw will speed the work considerably, as will an electric drill. But you can use hand tools, as opposed to power tools, most successfully. Ideally, here is what you should have to build the table: an electric handsaw, an electric drill with a 5/16″ bit, a metal framing square, a hammer, a steel tape measure and an adjustable wrench. A router is ideal for turning the edges on the benches and the table and will give the finished job a more professional look. Sanding, however, will work just as well, so don't go out and buy a $75 router if you don't already have one!

All ten boards will fit into the trunk of a car; at least, that's the way I got mine home. Since you're using ordinary building-grade lumber, I suggest you accompany the fellow at the lumberyard and pick out fairly decent boards. Avoid those boards that already show cracks and knotholes. Also, sight down the length of the boards and make sure they're reasonably straight. If you tell the lumberyard people what you intend to do with the lumber, they'll be helpful.

Now that you have all ten boards stacked up in the backyard, pick out the five best boards and set them aside. These five boards are destined to become the top and the benches of the table. Check the length of those five boards and make sure they measure exactly 8'. If not, trim them down.

The boards are all approximately 8' in length, which translates to 96". Take one of the five remaining boards and using a framing square, mark it off in three lengths of 32". Cut the 32" lengths and set the three boards aside. These three boards will serve to hold the top of the table together and keep it from excessive warping. Next, you'll want to cut the center brace of the table. Take another 8' board and cut it to exactly 68".

Now you're ready to cut the legs and the seat braces. Don't be afraid of the angle cut that is required! The framing square is designed for this type of job, and it is simple to use. Take another 8' board and place it on a sawhorse. Use the framing square to determine the angle by placing the metal square on top of the board. Notice that the square is numbered like a ruler and can, in fact, be used as one. One leg of the square will be longer than the other. Locate the numeral 12 along the outer edge of the shorter leg of the square and the numeral 6 on the outer edge of the other leg. When these two numbers of the square are aligned with the edge of the board, you will have the precise angle necessary.

Legs and Braces

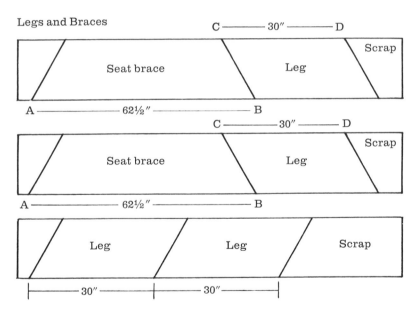

To cut out the end sections of the table, use a framing square to determine the angle. The shorter length of the framing square is called the tongue. Locate the numeral 12 along the front edge of the tongue and align 12 with the edge of the board. The other length of the framing square is called the blade. Find the numeral 6 along the front edge of the blade and align that number with the same front edge of the board. Now check and make sure that 12 and 6 are both as shown in the photo.

You will save material if you cut one seat brace and one leg from each of two 8′ boards. Start at one end of the board and align your framing square for the proper angle. The seat braces are 62½″ in length and the legs are 30″. Since the board is 96″ long, you'll have a couple of inches to spare.

Make your first angle about 1″ from the end of the board. Next, measure 62½″ from point "A" to point "B." Then use the same method in determining your angle. Next, measure 30″ from point "C" to point "D," and determine your angle the same as before. Cut along the marked angles and you will have one seat brace and one leg from an 8′ length of material. Repeat the process with another board. Then use the last board for two additional 30″ legs.

Now you're ready to assemble the table. Start with the top. Lay out the three boards that you have selected for the tabletop, with the less perfect side, if there is one, facing up. Space them at least ½″ apart; this space will allow rain, snowmelt, etc., to run off the table instead of standing in pools.

Next, locate the exact center of the top, which should be 4′ in from each end. At this center point, lay one of the 32″ lengths of two-by-twelve, which are in fact braces, across the tabletop boards at a right angle. The braces will be bolted to the top, but for the time being it's necessary to use nails to hold the assembly together. Drive a couple of nails to secure each board in position. Then measure in 2½″ from each end of the tabletop, lay the end braces across it and nail them in place.

Next, turn the top over before you drill the holes for the bolts. An electric drill will tend to tear the wood when the bit breaks through the hole. With the tabletop right side up, the tear will occur on the underside, where it won't show. I suggest that you put four bolts into each board. It

Draw a pencil line down the blade of the framing square, and then cut along that line.

may look like bridge construction, but it will keep the table boards from warping. Drill the holes and then insert the bolts so that the head of the bolt is exposed on the top of the table. Push the bolt into place; then whack it with a hammer and it will countersink flush with the top. Use a flat washer and nut on the underside of the table, and employing a wrench, draw the nut very tight. Altogether, it will take thirty-six bolts to hold the tabletop to its braces.

Next comes the assembly of the legs. This isn't tough, but it can be tricky, so follow my instructions and the illustrations carefully! First, take the two boards that are to be the legs, measure 8½″ with the angle and mark. Next, take one of the seat braces, measure 11½″ from each end and make a mark. Now, place the seat brace on top of the two legs. Align the marks on the legs with the bottom edge of the seat brace; just doing this will give you the proper height and angle. Now move the legs apart until they align with the 11½″ marks on the seat brace. The tops of the legs will not be together. Drill two holes through each leg and the seat brace and bolt into place.

Now you must attach a two-by-two wood cleat to the top of the legs. If you have not already cut the 10′ length of two-by-two, do so now. You will need two pieces 24″ long and six pieces 11″ long.

Attach the 24″ length of two-by-two to the tops of the legs by drilling two holes into each leg and through the two-by-two. This cleat will help stiffen the legs and will also serve to hold the top to the legs. After the cleat is attached to the legs, four holes must be drilled through the cleat to allow the leg assembly to be bolted to the top. These holes should be drilled now so that you will avoid the possibility of drilling into the bolts that hold the cleat to the legs when you attach the tabletop.

Next, you must attach two of the 11″ cleats to the seat brace. These cleats will enable you to bolt the seat boards to the seat braces. Attach the cleats to the seat brace by drilling two holes and inserting the bolts. Next, drill two other holes vertically through the cleat so that the seat board can be bolted on. Trimming the ends of the cleat to the contour of the seat brace will make for a nicer-looking job.

Now you must attach another 11″ cleat to each leg assembly to hold the center support of the table in place. The drawing of the leg assembly shows the location of this cleat. Find the center of the seat brace, and bolt one cleat in place on each leg assembly. Then drill two other holes, shown by broken lines, which will be used to bolt on the center brace.

Now the center brace is ready to be put in place. I found it a help, in doing this job alone, to use temporary nails to hold things in position. Putting the center brace in place

Measuring Leg Assembly

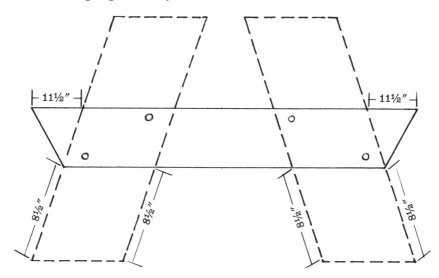

Assemble the top first. The top is made of three 8' lengths of 2" x 12" board. The crosspieces are designed to keep the top from warping. Each brace is 32" long, and each one is held in place by 12 ¼" bolts, each bolt 3½" long.

1 A completed leg assembly.
2 This is the 24″ two-by-two cleat that will hold the top of the table to the leg assembly.

1   2

1 One of the 11″ two-by-two cleats designed to hold the benches to the leg assemblies.
2 Another wood cleat, this one designed for the center brace of the table.

Leg Assembly

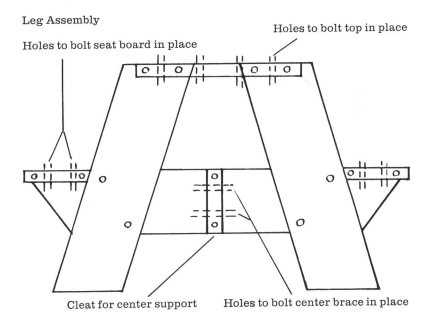

Holes to bolt seat board in place

Holes to bolt top in place

Cleat for center support   Holes to bolt center brace in place

is one of those examples. Place one end of the center brace against the cleat that has already been bolted to the leg assembly. Drive a nail through the center brace into the cleat. Now do the same thing with the other leg assembly. This makes it much easier to drill the holes that will be used to bolt the center brace to the cleats. Place the drill in the hole already drilled in the cleat and continue the hole through the center brace; then bolt in place.

Now for the top. Place the already assembled top on the leg assemblies. It will sort of position itself because of the braces on the underside of the top, but center the top over the legs. Now, complete drilling the holes through the cleats on the tops of the legs and through the tabletop itself. Four bolts will be more than adequate to attach the top to each leg assembly.

The final touch is adding the two benches. Position them on the seat braces, and drill your holes through the cleats into the bench itself. Two bolts are enough in each seat brace to hold things together. You can tip the table on its side to finish tightening the bolts.

I completed the job on my table by giving it two coats of exterior redwood stain. Putting some sort of protective finish on the table is imperative. Exterior finishes will help to seal the wood and keep it from checking, cracking and warping. It is important to apply the finish to all parts of the table, even the underside!

I know the instructions may sound complicated, but I assure you it took me longer to write this chapter than it did to build the table! It really is quite simple. Keep the illustrations and photos handy and you'll do the job in under four hours. (Even Natalie admits that this project is a real winner!)

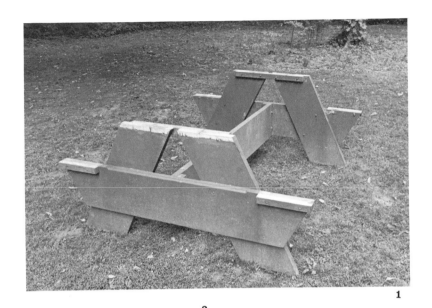

1

2

1 The assembled legs and center brace are now ready for the top and the benches.
2 Place the top on the already assembled legs, finish drilling the holes into the top, then hammer the bolts into place so that their heads are flush with the top of the table.

1 Tip the table up on its side to tighten the bolts under the top and under the benches.

2 There we are! It will seat ten people, and it will never tip over.

1

2

23 OUTDOOR STORAGE BUILDING

I had never even tried to build an outdoor storage building until it became apparent that this would be a good subject for **Wally's Workshop.** I looked around several lumber-yards for plans, but none of those offered was the sort of building you could assemble in the sixteen minutes we have on television. That's when I sort of designed my own, and today it is in my backyard serving quite well.

My storage building was constructed out of five sheets of ¾" exterior plywood, a bundle of 1" x 2" furring strips and a couple of dozen screen-door hooks and eyes. I wanted to demonstrate the kind of building that would offer either temporary or permanent storage facilities for a lawn mower and garden tools or even double as a playhouse for the kids. Since not everyone owns their own home, I also wanted the building to be movable and to come apart as easily as it goes together. Also, since it is not a permanent structure, you can outfox the tax assessor.

The overall dimensions of the building are as follows: width, 4'; length, 6'; height at front, 6'; height at back, 5'. The building has a shed-type roof with a 1' drop from front to back. You'll notice in the pictures that I used one-by-

1 This lovely lass is Natalie, who is holding the two sides in place while I'm looking for the end section.

2 Notice that I cut the end section just a few inches shorter than the sides to provide for a bit of ventilation. Storing gasoline, etc., can be dangerous in a tightly sealed building.

1

2

twos around the edges of each section to straighten the plywood and also to give me a better material in which to set the screws and screw eyes.

The only tools needed are a saw, hammer, pliers and a chalk line or straightedge. I am willing to guarantee that you can cut out and assemble the building in under three hours. It isn't essential to use screen-door hooks and eyes; if you want a more permanent structure, use nails and glue (Never omit glue!). After it's assembled, make sure you give the plywood some sort of protective coating. A couple of coats of paint will do it; so will some of the wood sealer/preservatives.

I guess I really don't expect everyone to follow my exact plans for an outdoor storage building, but this one may start you off in the right direction to design your own. Try to design a building to utilize the standard dimensions of the material available. For example, I made my storage building 6′ in length, which meant I used one and one-half sheets of 4′ x 8′ plywood for each side. I only had to make one cut, and there wasn't any waste except the part I cut off at the roof line.

Build this one or one of your own design—but remember, you can do it if you try!

Natalie's Notes

Now, this is not the most glamorous edifice imaginable, as you can see from the photos, but then, neither is the overweight female model. (I pleaded with W. B. not to use the pictures!) My contribution to the project consisted solely of holding up the sections while Wally put them together. I offered to cut a big crescent moon on the door, but was turned down.

 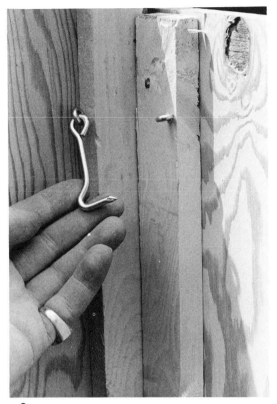

1   2

1 Notice how I recessed the one-by-two furring strip so that the other section will butt into this one.
2 See how simply it all fits together? The hooks should fit as tightly as possible into the eyes. If the building is to be permanent, skip the hooks and nail it together.

1 Hooks and eyes like this one should
be installed at four points on the
end panel, four points on the front
panel and four points on the roof
section.
2 Once the end section is hooked on,
the building will stand by itself.
With a little help, lift the 4′ x 8′ roof
section into place.

1

2

1

2

1 I split the overhang of the roof into front and rear, and it too is attached by hooks and eyes.
2 Another 4′ x 8′ sheet makes the fully removable front door, and as you can see, Sam, our German shepherd, is ready to move right in!

OUTDOOR STORAGE BUILDING   251